Lee Genud's
BACKGAMMON
BOOK

by Lee Genud

**CLIFF
HOUSE
BOOKS**
LOS ANGELES

Distributed by Price/ Stern/ Sloan Publishers, Inc. Los Angeles

A Cliff House— P/S/S Book
Second Printing - September 1975

Published by Cliff House Books
Distributed by Price/Stern/Sloan Publishers, Inc.
410 North La Cienega Boulevard, Los Angeles, California 90048
Printed in the United States of America. All rights reserved.
ISBN: 0-8431-0342-6

ACKNOWLEDGEMENTS

I wish to acknowledge the many people who have helped me with this book: Andi Kennard, without whom I would never have made my deadlines, my good friend and editor Jack S Margolis, who conceived the idea of this book, Roger Bates and Danny Romm, for their help, "Chouette," my beautiful cat, who was purchased from my first tournament winnings (which made all this possible), and with special thanks to Manny Wong, who helped me cover my blots, to Stanley Tomchin who taught me when to leave them, and to Sara Bates who helped me write about them.

TABLE OF CONTENTS

TABLE OF CONTENTS

CHAPTER 1

BASIC RULES

Do you remember that strange-looking square with the black and red points on the other side of the checkerboard that you played with as a kid? That "other side," which has so long been a doormat to Parker Bros. checker sets, is a backgammon board. Turn over your tired old board, find your plastic checkers (use old poker chips for the ones the kids lost) and settle down for an introduction to the ancient and venerable game of backgammon.

The basic requirements are:

1) A backgammon board.
2) Two players.
3) A pair of dice. If you can scrounge up two pair, that would be even better.
4) Thirty men or checkers. There should be 15 of one color and 15 of another color. For our purposes we will use black and white throughout the book.
5) Cube. The doubling cube is to backgammon what the raise is to poker. It is the large "fifth" die in your set and its faces are numbered with 2, 4, 8, 16, 32, and 64. It is used to raise the stakes of the game and to indicate the score. More about this in Chapter V.
6) A clear head. Send your ego out for an errand. It will only get in your way and deprive you of a lot of I.Q. points that you can't afford to waste.

Diagram #1 illustrates the board in the original starting position. You will begin each game in this manner and may refer to this diagram until you have the position memorized.

Diagram #1

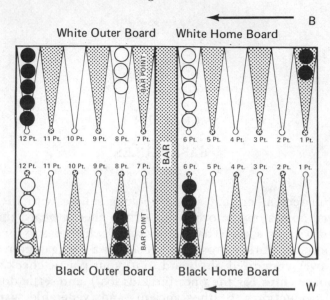

The board is divided into four quadrants or tables. Each table has six triangular "points" of alternating colors, or 24 points in all. The points alternate in color to help you count your moves.

The points in the inner (or home) board or table are numbered from one to six, and those in the outer table are numbered from seven to twelve. The dividing space between the inner and outer tables is called the "bar."

The object of the game is to *first* bring all of your men into your home board, and *then* to remove them from the table (called "bearing off"). The person who gets all of his men off the table first wins.

Your men, black, will move counter-clockwise around the boards to your inner or home table. Your opponent's men, white, will move in the opposite direction (clockwise) to his home table. The board may be said to be a battlefield with two armies fighting to pass each other and get home.

Each person in turn rolls two dice, and moves his men according to the number of each die. You may move a different man for each die, or one man may move the numbers of both die, touching down on the board after the first number.

Thus if you roll a 5-4, you can move one man five points and another man four points, or you can move the same man five and then four or four and then five points.

You may also take back any move you make, and make another, until you remove your dice from the board.

With these basic concepts in mind, you're ready to begin to play. The following discussion will be easier to understand if you follow along on your own board. If you or your opponent have any psychic penchant for the same color of men and direction of movement (the board may be set up in a "mirror image" to the way we've depicted it and you should learn both ways) the matter may be settled by a simple roll of the dice. The high roll gets his way and hopefully no fistfights break out.

To begin the actual play, each man rolls one die and the man with the high die moves first, using the numbers on these two dice as his first roll. Thus, if black rolls a six and white rolls a three, black has the first move of 6-3. Black may use one man to move six points and another man to move three points, or he may use one man to make both moves, touching down after moving either six or three points.

If you both roll the same number, continue to roll until you each roll a different one. No game can begin with doubles. After this first roll, each man rolls his two dice on his turn. If possible, you must play both numbers of any roll. If you can move only one of the two numbers, you must choose the higher number. Sometimes you will be forced to make an uncomfortable move, leaving blots like sitting ducks all over the board. In a forced situation the best strategy is to move quickly, act confident, and hope for the best.

TYPES OF WINS:

In backgammon you have a chance to win not only a single game, but a double or triple game. If you win a single game your opponent has taken off at least one of his men before you have taken off all of yours. A double game or "gammon" is icing on the cake. It occurs when you have taken off all of your men before your opponent has removed any of his. A triple game or "backgammon" is rubbing salt in the wound. It occurs when your opponent has taken off *none of his men* and has one or more of his men either in your home table or on the bar when you have taken off *all* of your men. Don't gloat; he may backgammon you in the next game.

9

DOUBLES:

Any time after the first roll of the game a double number (the same number on each die) is to be played by moving four times the number on *one* die. For example, a double three may be played by:

a) moving one man a total of twelve points
b) moving two men six points each
c) moving one man three points and another man nine points
d) moving two men three points each and a third man six points
e) moving four men three points each.

BAR:

The bar is the center raised strip of the board that separates the outer and inner boards. A checker that is hit (more about this in a moment) is placed on the bar until it can legally re-enter your opponent's home board.

BLOT:

A single man on a point is called a blot. When a blot is hit by your opponent (that is, when your opponent lands or touches down on that point) that man must go to the bar, re-enter on an open point (one that doesn't have two or more of your opponent's men on it) in your opponent's home board and begin again. The man or men on the bar must re-enter before you are allowed to move any other men on the board.

POINT:

A point is any of the 24 triangles. You may put a man on any point that is not occupied by two or more of your opponent's men. There is no limit to how many of your own men you may put on one point. Most backgammon players use the term "pip" instead of point when referring to the relationship between points. Thus, the eight point is one pip from the seven point, or if you roll a ten, and then get hit, you've wasted ten pips.

MAKING A POINT:

When you have two or more of your men on a point, you "own" that point (or have "made" that point) and your opponent can not land or touch down on that point. Making a point has nothing to do with the scoring of the game, and I wish, for purposes of clarity, that it was termed a "block" rather than "making a point." When you make a point, you both protect your own men and block your opponent's men.

To illustrate this, in Diagram #2 white owns his six, seven and eight points (and, of course, black's one and twelve points). Black rolls a 6-3.

Diagram #2

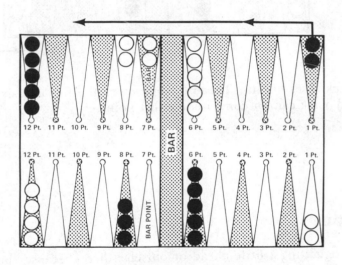

In order to legally move a 6-3 from white's one point to white's ten point, black must first move a three and then a six. He cannot move a six first, because he would touch down on the seven point (also known as the "Bar Point") which white owns. If black rolls double sixes from the same position, he cannot move at all from the one point. He would have to make his move elsewhere on the board.

In Diagram #3, black is on the bar and rolls a 6-5.

11

Diagram #3

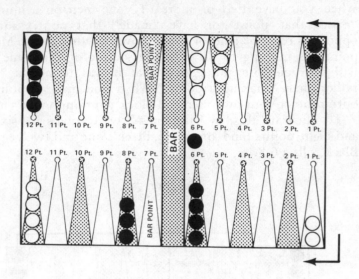

Black loses his turn because white owns the five and six points and black cannot come in on either point.

PRIME:

We're getting a little ahead of ourselves here because "building a prime" has to do with strategy rather than rules, but it shows you the importance of "making a point." Making three or more adjacent points is called a "prime." Since you want to impede your opponent's progress and move your men around the table before he does, you can easily see that if you build a six point prime with some of your opponent's men trapped behind it, you've stopped those men completely (at least until you have to break up your prime). In Diagram #4, there is no roll or combination of rolls that will allow white to escape black's prime.

Diagram #4

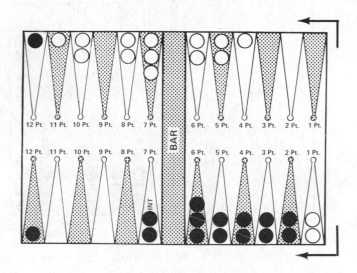

White must therefore make all of his moves elsewhere on the board until black is forced to break up his prime.

BEARING OFF:

When all of your men have entered your home board, you may begin taking them off the board, or "bearing off." You bear your men off from the points corresponding to the numbers on the roll of the dice. You may either move a man forward in your inner board or bear off. In Diagram #5, black rolls a 4-3.

Diagram #5

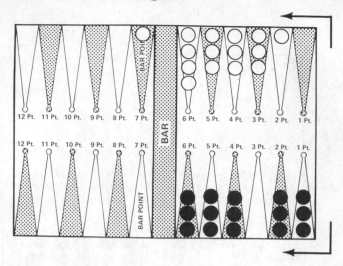

Black may take a man off the four point. Since he has no man on the three point, he must move a man from the six point to the three point, or a man from the five point to the two point.

When you roll a number higher than any covered point, you may bear off from the highest covered point.

In Diagram #6, black rolls a 6-4.

Diagram #6

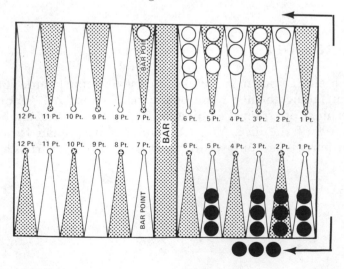

Since Black has no man on the six point, he must bear a man off the five point. He still must move his four from the five point to the one point.

If, while bearing off, one of your men is hit, he must go to the bar, re-enter, and travel around to your home board before you take off any of your other men.

In Diagram #7, white rolls a 5-2.

Diagram #7

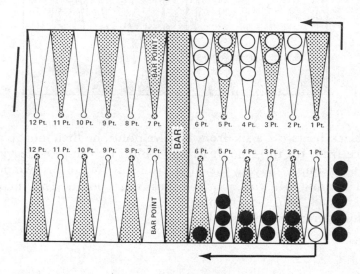

He hits black with a five. Black must now re-enter white's home board and return to his own home board before he bears off any more of his men.

Some bear-off positions can be very deceptive. It is important to consider all possibilities of the roll because the correct play is often the least obvious one.

In Diagram #8, black rolls a 6-3.

Diagram #8

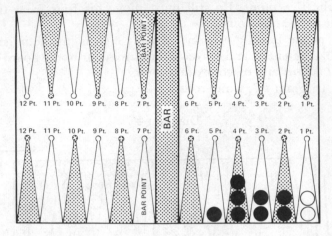

If black bears off a six from his five point, he then must play a three from his three point leaving a blot. He can avoid leaving a blot by simply playing the three from his five to his two point and bearing off the six from his four point. This play is nicknamed "burying a number."

In Diagram #9, black rolls a 5-2.

Diagram #9

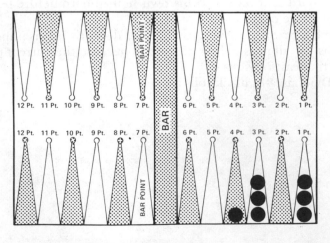

If black plays the five to bear off from his four point, he must then scoot a two to his one point (leaving men on his one and three points only). Yet, if he plays the two from his four to his two point, he may then use the five to bear off from his three point (leaving men on his one, two and three points) and have a two to play on his next roll. In these and other similar situations, always look at the roll both ways before making your play.

CHAPTER II

BASIC STRATEGY

TYPES OF STRATEGY:

There are three general types of strategy which develop early in the game, and one of these becomes your general plan of attack throughout the play. It is likely that your course will be altered somewhat by your opponent's game and the whim of the dice, but it is a good idea to have a game plan in mind.

RUNNING:

The most basic type of strategy is the running game. If, having rolled high numbers, you find yourself ahead in the race position, you should play a running game. Try to avoid contact and win the game by virtue of higher dice. A beginner, having little skill, may try to make every game into a running game.

BLOCKING:

Another type of game develops if you have begun the game by establishing a series of points in your inner and outer boards. You thereby block your opponent's men by foiling any of his attempts to escape. This is called a blocking game. If things go well you can combine the above game with this one and come up with a very effective race-block game. This is probably the strongest type of approach.

BACK GAME:

The third type of game evolves from a blot-hitting contest. The game begins with you and your opponent landing on each others' blots and sending them to the bar. When the smoke clears, one player has gained an advantage and begins to play more safely. The other player, as a result of having been hit so often, may hold two or more points in his opponent's inner board. He has developed a defensive game commonly known as the "back game." A back game is the most difficult game to play or defend and will be discussed in full in Chapter VI.

OPENING MOVES:

Having the opening move gives you the offensive edge in the early game. It is of crucial importance for you to employ that edge to your best advantage. Some opening rolls are clearly good rolls and there is no dispute as to the move to be taken, and there are some very bad opening rolls with only one good but generally undisputed way to move them. Then there are the mediocre rolls with some options as to how to move them. These rolls we have indicated with an asterisk to list the alternatives. The plays are often equally good and the way you choose to play them becomes a matter of style. It is important for you to memorize the opening moves. Don't despair; they'll soon become automatic.

You will often hear the terms "splitting" and "slotting" in backgammon jargon. For those in the know, they have special meaning. When I explain the opening move of a 2-1, 4-1, or 5-1, I give two ways to play each roll. In all three moves the first number (two, four or five) is played the same way, but the one may be played one of two ways. The first option I've listed, moving a man from your opponent's one point to his two point, is called "splitting" because you're splitting up the two back men. The second play, moving a man from your six to your five point, is called "slotting." The term "slotting" means putting a man on an empty point in the hopes of making the point on your next roll. Your choice of moves is entirely a matter of personal preference. Slotting is certainly the more aggressive play since you leave your opponent a nice juicy target to hit, and he will hit this blot 15 out of 36 times.

However, if the blot survives on your next roll you will cover

18

it with ones, threes, and eights at least and make your extremely valuable five point. If you decide to split, you greatly reduce your chances of making a point in your home board and you reduce the likelihood of becoming involved in a blot-hitting contest. When you split, your advantage lies in putting the pressure on your opponent's outer board and increasing the probabilities of making a point in his inner board. Although I generally slot, I suggest that you split until you become proficient enough to handle a complicated blot-hitting contest.

OPENING ROLLS

White Outer   *White Home*

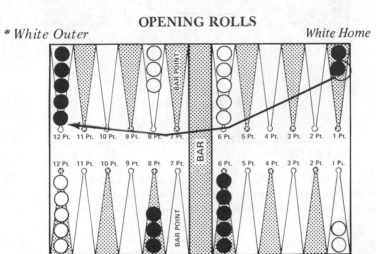

6-5: move a man from white's one point to white's 12 point.

White Outer   *White Home*

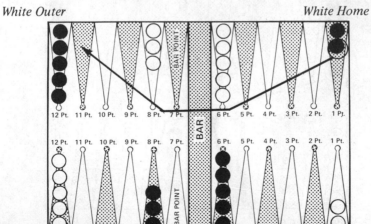

6-4: move a man from white's one point to white's 11 point.

19

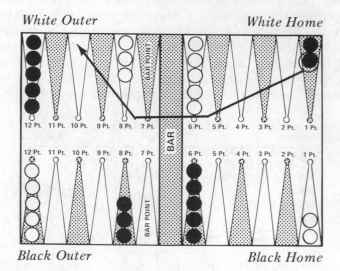

6-3: move a man from white's one point to white's 10 point.
* move a man from white's one point to white's bar point, and move
a man from white's 12 point to your 10 point.

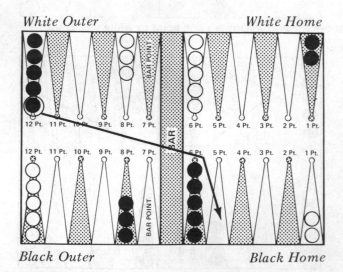

6-2: move a man from white's 12 point to your five point.

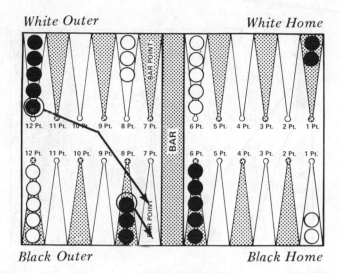

6-1: make your bar point. Move a man from white's **12** point to your bar point and a man from your eight point to your bar point.

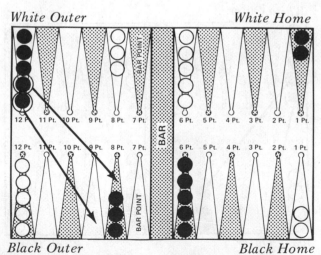

5-4: move two men from white's **12** point to your eight and nine points.

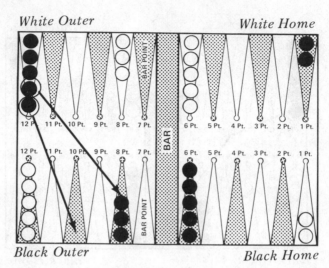

5-3: move two men from white's 12 point to your eight and 10 points.

* make your three point. Move a man from your eight point and one from your six point to your three point.

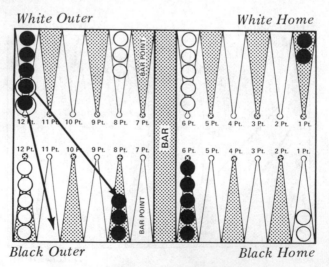

5-2: move two men from white's 12 point to your eight and 11 points.

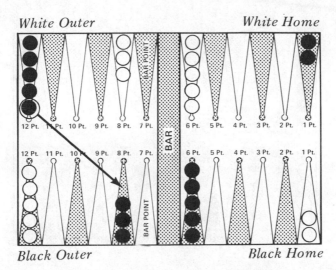

5-1: move one man from white 12 point to your eight point and one man from white one to white two point.

* move one man from white 12 point to your eight point and one man from your six point to your five point.

* alternate play

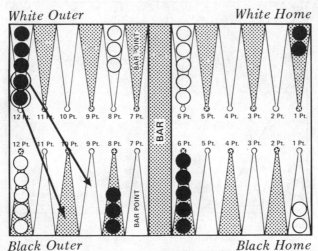

4-3: move two men from white **12** point to your nine and ten points.

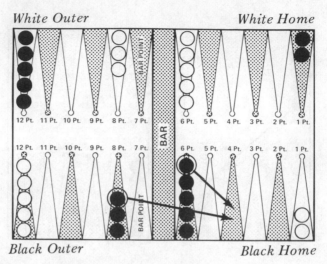

4-2: make your four point. Move one man from your eight point and one man from your six point to your four point.

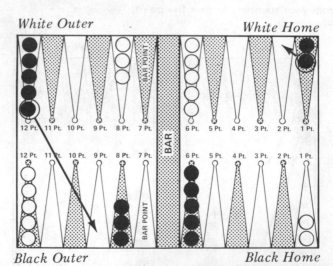

4-1: move one man from white 12 point to your nine point and one man from white one point to white two point.

* move one man from white 12 point to your nine point and one man from your 6 point to your 5 point.

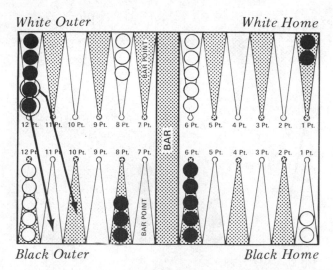

3-2: move two men from white 12 point to your 10 and 11 points.

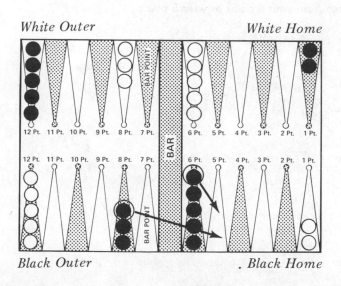

3-1: make your 5 point. Move one man from your 8 point and one man from your 6 point to your 5 point.

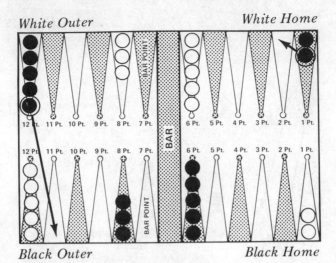

2-1: move one man from white 12 point to your 11 point and move one man from white 1 point to white 2 point.
* move one man from white 12 point to your 11 point and move one man from your 6 point to your 5 point.

26

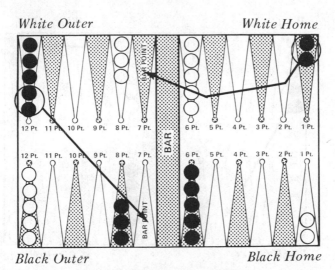

Double 6: Make both bar points. Move two men from white one point to white bar point, and two men from white 12 point to your bar point.

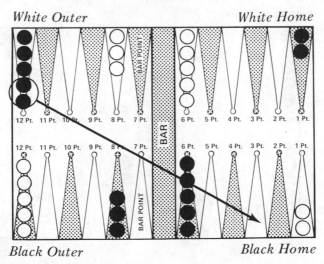

Double 5: Make your three point. Move two men from white 12 point to your three point.

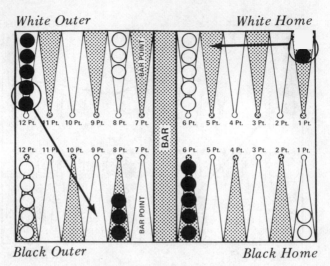

Double 4: Move two men from white one point to white five point and two men from white 12 point to your nine point.
* Move two men from white 12 point to your five point.

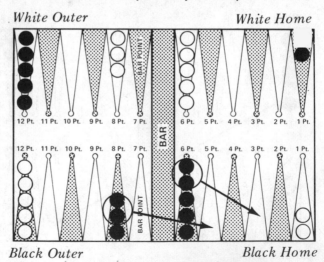

Double 3: Make your five and three points. Move two men from your eight point to your five point and two men from your six point to your three point.
* Move two men from white 12 point to your bar point.

* alternate play

28

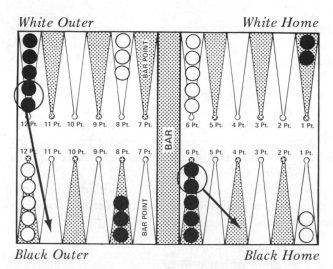

White Outer   *White Home*

Black Outer   *Black Home*

Double 2: Make your four and 11 points. Move two men from your six point to your four point and two men from white 12 point to your 11 point.

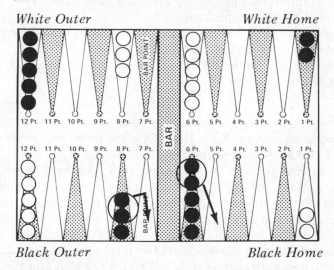

White Outer   *White Home*

Black Outer   *Black Home*

Double 1: Make your bar and five points. Move two men from your eight point to your bar point, and move two men from your six point to your five point.

REPLY TO THE OPENING MOVE:

Hopefully, you have learned your opening rolls before you read this section. You will find it much easier to follow this discussion if you have a knowledge of the plays to which we will reply.

You are now in the position of making the second play of the game. This play, as well as all others, depends upon the move your opponent has already made. The board now becomes a battlefield and you are the general maneuvering your forces to the best advantage. Keep in mind your objective and use your best judgment to achieve that end.

In making his opening move your opponent has done one of several things. There are five classifications in which the opening move will fall. Your opponent will have:

1) made an inner or bar point.
2) brought men from your outer board to his outer board as "builders" to make such a point.
3) attempted to run one of his back men from your inner board to your outer board.
4) split his back men in your inner board and brought a builder down to his outer board.
5) slotted a man in his inner board and brought a builder down to his outer board.

There are several principles involved in the reply to any of these opening tactics. Keep these in mind when you make your play. If you must leave a blot:

1) *Leave as few direct shots as possible.* A blot that is within a six point range of one of your opponent's men is vulnerable to a direct shot. In other words, he can be hit by a specific number of a single die on any given roll. If a blot is within a 7-12 point range of one of your opponent's men, he is vulnerable to an indirect or combination shot. In this case a combination number using both dice is required to hit the blot and the odds of being hit are greatly decreased. I will go into specific probabilities later in the book, but keep in mind this basic concept.

30

2) *Leave your blot where it will be most effective if it is not hit.* If you survive your opponent's roll and are not hit, you want to use that blot to your maximum advantage.

In Diagram #10, black rolls a 6-4.

Diagram #10

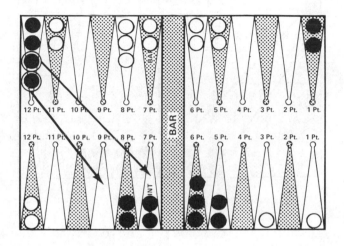

He plays a six safely from his opponent's twelve point to his bar point. Now he has to decide where to play a four. He must leave a blot. If he plays a four from his six point to his two point, he leaves a direct one. If he moves a four from his opponent's twelve point to his nine point, he leaves a direct six or a combination 5-1. This is the correct play. If he is not hit and rolls a four on his next roll, he will make a five point prime and block white's back men. He has also left himself more combinations to make an inner point on his next roll.

3) *Leave a blot where it is uncomfortable for your opponent to hit you.*

In Diagram #11, black again rolls a 6-4.

31

Diagram #11

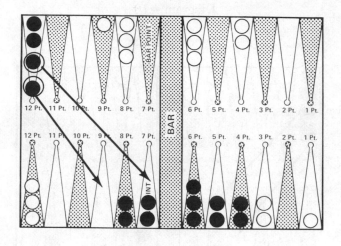

Black safely plays a six from his opponent's twelve point to his own bar point. He may play a four from his six point to his two point, leaving a direct one, or he may play a four from his opponent's twelve point to his nine point, leaving a direct six. The latter is the correct play. If white is to hit black on his nine point, he must leave the safety of his anchor on black's three point, leaving himself vulnerable to be "closed out" by black. Since white doesn't have many points in his board, black can well afford to take the risk.

4) *Hit two blots whenever possible.* This incapacitates your opponent for a minimum of one roll (with the exception of doubles) and gives you time to deploy your men without risk. *EXAMPLES:* I will defend five opening rolls by considering the replies to a typical move of each type.

1) 3-1: In Diagram #12, my opponent (white) rolls a 3-1 and makes his five point.

Diagram #12

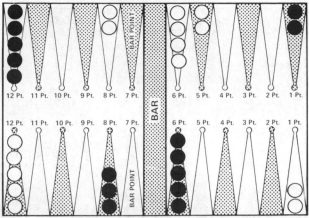

He has made the most valuable point in his board and begun the game with a very strong position. I don't want to be hit with the threat of a two point board, and I would like to get my back men out as soon as possible. I have no threat to keep my opponent from taking a few chances to improve his position. I roll in reply:

a) Double 4:   I can't move my back men up so I will make my five point. It is a good roll and I now have as strong a position as my opponent.

b) Double 3:   This is an excellent roll. My prime consideration is to move my back men up to my opponent's four point where I am secure in the knowledge that I won't be trapped. I will also make my five point. I now have a two-way threat on my opponent: I am beginning to block his back men and I am bearing down on his outer board.

c) 6-2: Normally, I would slot a man on my five point, but that play looks a little aggressive now. Instead, I will run a man from my opponent's one point to his nine point. I will be hit here with a four, but if he misses, I will have escaped with one man. If I am hit, I won't have wasted as many pips by running the back man as I would by slotting my five point.

d)   5-1, 4-1 and 2-1: I will split my back man from my opponent's one point to his two point instead of slotting on my five point. This play serves a dual purpose: I reduce my chances of being hit and I maximize my chances for escape.

2)   4-3: In Diagram #13, my opponent rolls a 4-3 and brings down two builders to his nine and ten points.

Diagram #13

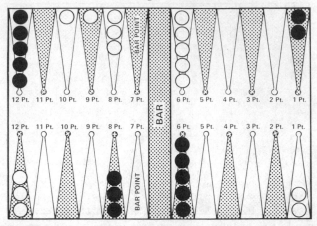

I roll in reply:

a) Double 4: As always, I look to see if there is a blot to be hit. There is, and now I must consider whether or not to hit. Most often I will and this is no exception to the rule. I move a man from my opponent's one point to his nine point and put a man on the bar. I now have two fours left to play and I have to decide where they will do my opponent the most harm. Since he has a man on the bar, I will make my four point. This lessens his chances of coming in to my board from the bar.

3) 6-3: In Diagram #14, my opponent rolls a 6-3 and runs a man from my one point to my ten point.

Diagram #14

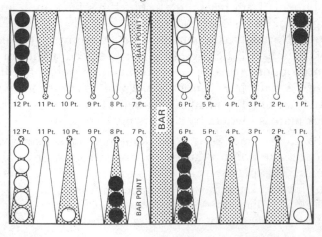

34

I roll in reply:

a) Double 5: This roll becomes a little more palatable than usual. I tend to make my one and three points, putting white on the bar, although in doing so I am almost committed to trying to make all my home board points (called a "closeout position").

b) Double 3: This is just what I ordered. I bring two men from my opponent's twelve point to my ten point, putting a man on the bar. I then make my five point.

c) 6-4: I won't make my normal running play with this roll because then I would be exposed to a hit by both twos and fours. I have two options on this play. I will bring a four down from my opponent's twelve point to my nine point and either play the six to my bar or my opponent's bar. If I take it to my bar I leave fewer shots, but I also lose many more pips if I am hit. The play becomes a matter of style and I can't quarrel with either play.

d) 6-3: I hit the man on my ten point with the three, and use the six to move a man from my opponent's one point to his bar point.

e) 2-1: I use the full number to hit the blot on my ten point.

f) 5-2: If I make my normal play here, I leave a blot on my eleven point exposed to a one and a 6-4. The odds make me a favorite not to be hit, but I also have an alternative play: I can split from my opponent's one point to his three point, although this play turns double fives, 3-2, or 5-3 into dream rolls for my opponent. Yet if he doesn't annihilate me, I exert a great amount of pressure on his outer board. Either play is reasonable, since the roll is about the worst.

g) 3-1: I would hit the blot on my ten point with the three and split my back men with the one. I would make the five point in these situations only if my opponent still has two men back, since then his chances of escape would be minimal.

4) 4-1: In Diagram #15 my opponent rolls a 4-1. He splits his back men from my one point to my two point, and plays a four from my twelve to his nine point.

Diagram #15

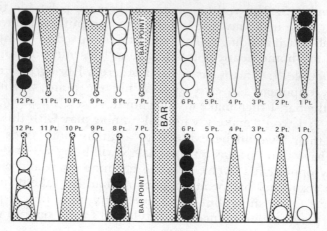

I roll in reply:

a)   Double 5: I make my three point and either hit on my one point and leave a blot there, or I make my one point. If I make the point, I have put two of my men out of play, and I am committed to a closeout position. If I leave the blot (and move my fourth five from my opponent's twelve point to cover the blot on my eight point), I may be able to get the man back into play where he is more effective. This would happen if my opponent hits me coming in from the bar. There is a lot to be said for either play and it will probably be debated by experts until the end of time.

b)   6-2, 5-3: I hit the blot on the nine point with one of my back men.

c)   5-1, 4-1 and 2-1: Since my opponent has split his back men, I don't ever slot the one on my five point. He would then have two men bearing down on my blot and I would leave him a direct double shot. Instead I split my back men with the one and play the other number as a builder.

d)   4-3, 3-2: Since my opponent has two men bearing on my outer board, I will only bring down one man as a builder. I will split the three from my opponent's one point to his four point.

5)   4-1: In Diagram #16, my opponent rolls a 4-1. This time he makes the aggressive play, brings a man from my twelve point to his nine point and slots a man from his six to his five point. You will see how radically the reply to the same roll can change with the slot instead of the split.

Diagram #16

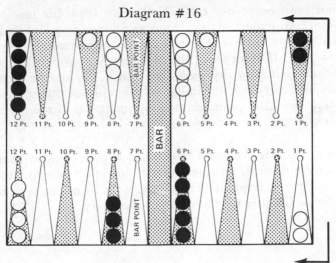

I roll in reply:

a) Double 4: The roll of the gods. I use one of my back men to hit the blots on my opponent's five and nine points. With two men on the bar it definitely seems right to make my four point.

b) Double 2: I hit the blot on my opponent's five point with one of my back men and make my four point.

c) 6-4: I make my normal running play, but on the way out I pick up the blot on my opponent's five point. Remember to take your four first or you lose the added attraction this roll now holds for you.

d) 5-3, 6-2: I hit the man on my opponent's nine point with one of my back men.

e) 5-4: I hit the man on my opponent's five point with the four and continue to move the man to my opponent's ten point with the five. I don't want my opponent to hit me on his five point on the return roll.

f) 4-3: I hit the man on my opponent's five point with the four and bring a man from his twelve to my ten point with the three as a builder.

g) 4-2: I hit the man on my opponent's five point with the four and bring a man from his twelve point to my eleven point with the two as a builder. Here it is more important to prevent him from making his five point than for me to make my four point.

h) 4-1: I hit the blot on my opponent's five point with the

37

four and move my other back man from his one to his two point. An expert may slot a man on his five point and leave the double shot if he is playing a weaker opponent.

i) 3-1: If I am to hit the blot on my opponent's five point, it means giving up my own five point. I'll hit the blot, but I'm paying dearly for it. Similar to the reply of the opening 6-3, I'll make my five point if my opponent has three or more men back, or two men to my one.

So far in this chapter I have boggled your mind with many new terms and ideas. I suggest that before you progress to the next chapter you implant the opening rolls firmly in your mind, and refer to Chapter One as often as necessary.

CHAPTER III

LET'S PLAY BACKGAMMON

Perhaps you have worn off the paint and paper points of your old backgammon-checker board while mastering the mechanics of the game. If you have, you are probably ready to buy a new set and begin to play in the big time.

If your opponent has been consistently beating you with double sixes in the bear-off, you may resent the idea of involving yourself further in this "lucky dice game" but stick with me. In this chapter I plan to show you that winning backgammon does indeed require a great deal of skill. You can learn to employ successfully the good, bad and mediocre rolls to whittle patiently away at your opponent's pocketbook, ego, or whatever else they have to offer.

No one rolls consistently better than anyone else, but some people play consistently better than others. I want my readers to learn not only to *rely* on the dice, but to *play* the dice.

The race game relies on the dice. If you depend on outrolling your opponent, you will win only half of the time, or not nearly often enough. The blocking game can make a simple race seem like child's play. It takes backgammon out of the sandbox and into the classroom and it becomes a game of wit, strategy and challenge.

In the following games, I have created a battlefield for the players to out hit, out block, and out race each other to victory.

BEGINNING RACE-BLOCK GAME:
This game is designed to give you practice with your opening rolls and basic strategy. Dust off your board and move the pieces with my friend Sara (black) and me (white) to familiarize yourself with the battlefield. Armed with the knowledge of opening moves and the desire to win the war, enjoy your trip into backgammon.

3-1

My favorite roll. Makes my 5 point with the men on my 8 and 6 points.

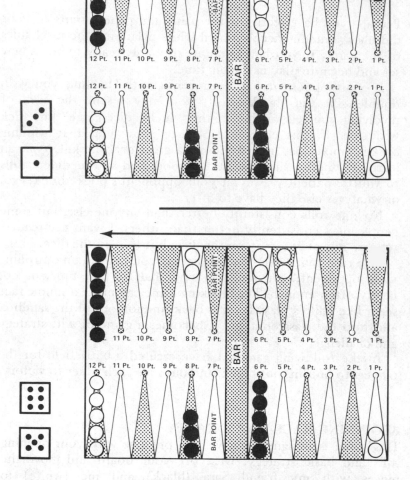

6-5

Lover's leap . . . can't forget that one. I move a man from Lee's 1 point to her 12 point, nice and safe.

4-2

Even though I must leave a blot on my 8 point susceptible to 6-1 and 5-2 (4 rolls out of 36) I will make my 4 point, giving me three points in a row.

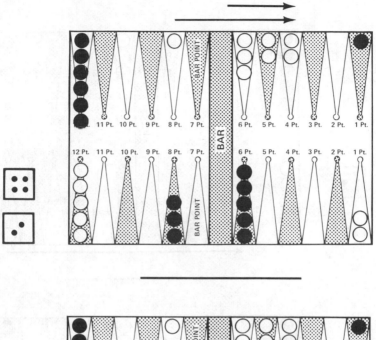

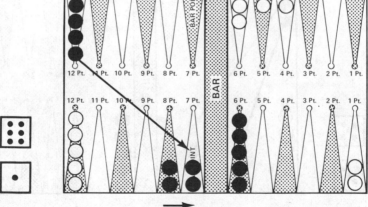

6-1

A man from Lee's 12 point to my bar, or 7 point, and a 1 from the 8 point to the bar . . . a good blocking position.

41

I'd like to get one of my imprisoned men from Sara's 1 point to her 10 point.

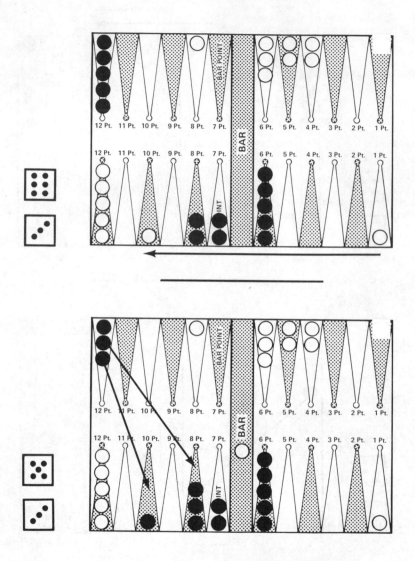

5-3

The three hits Lee's man on my 10 point and I'll move the 5 from Lee's 12 point to my 8 point.

5-4

A play designed for security. I'll come in on Sara's 5 point and move my man on her 1 point to the 5 point which gives me safety because it's unlikely she could make a prime while I'm as far forward as the 5 point. I'll be primed if she makes her 5 point.

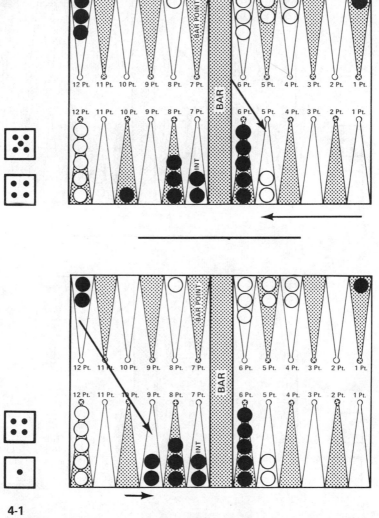

4-1

I could bring the man on the 10 point into my board but it's better to make the 9 point with a man from Lee's 12 point and a 1 from the 10 point. This gives me a 4 point prime, and helps to block Lee's men on my 5 point.

A good roll, makes a 4 point prime for me by making the bar.

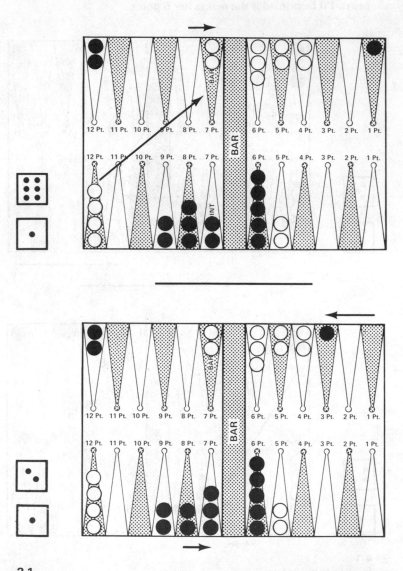

2-1

I needed that two, since my man on Lee's 1 point was stuck. I move up to the prime with the 2 so that I can exit with 5's and 6's and move a one from the eight to the seven point.

6-6

Box cars . . . and I'm on the move. Putting myself ahead in the race I move both men on Sara's 5 point all the way to my own 8 point.

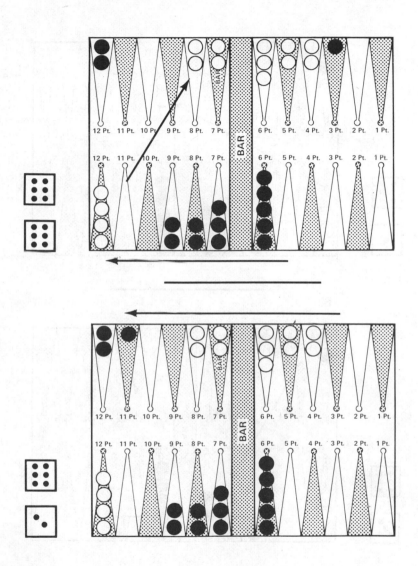

6-2

Time for escape . . . all the way with the man on Lee's 3 point out to her 11 point.

6-1
Happy to be racing, I bring a man from Sara's 12 point to my 6 point. The sooner my men get home, the sooner they come off the board.

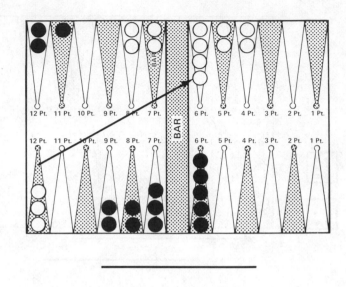

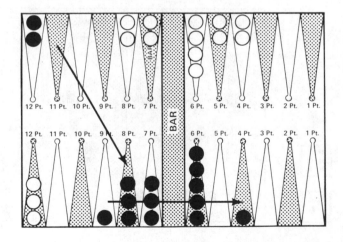

6-5
The six moves from Lee's 11 point to my 8 point and the 5 from the 9 to my 4 point.

4-1

The four gets me even on Sara's 12 point, also called the safety point, and the one is used to bring a man in. (Always use the least number of moves to get your men onto your home board.)

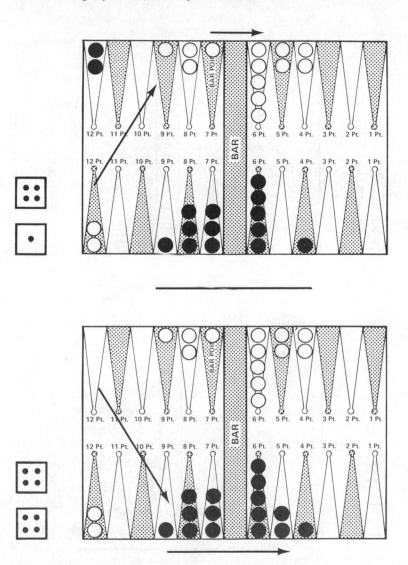

4-4

Whew! This race was frightening. I can bring the men on Lee's 12 point home to the 5 point. Not double sixes but surely not chopped liver either.

6-5

Two men across the board to my 7 and 8 points.

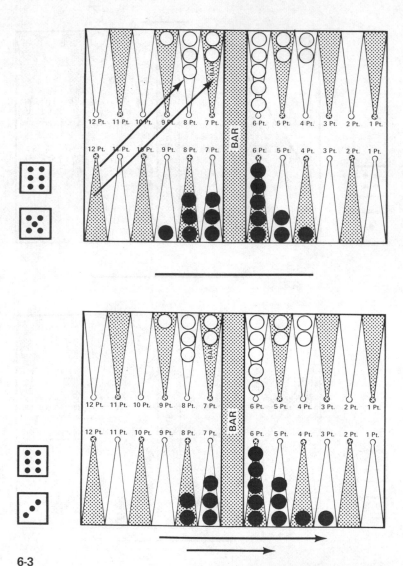

6-3

The six moves from my 9 point to my 3 and this brings a man from the 8 point to my 5 point. (If you're forced to waste points when moving men, waste the least number of points possible.

48

The five comes from my outside to the four point and the three from the eight to the five point.

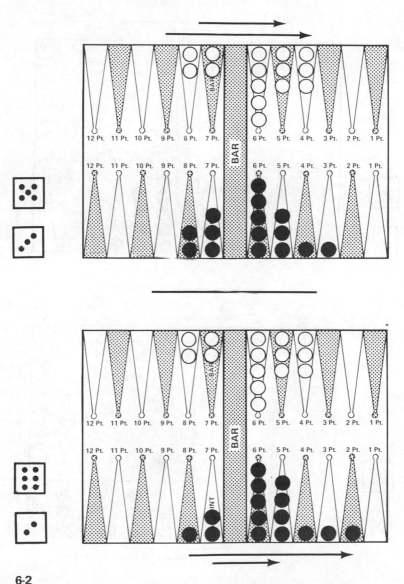

6-2
The six comes into the two and I will move the two to the five, instead of the six, because I already have a pile on the six point. (There seems to be an exception to every rule!)

Two men in again as advertised.

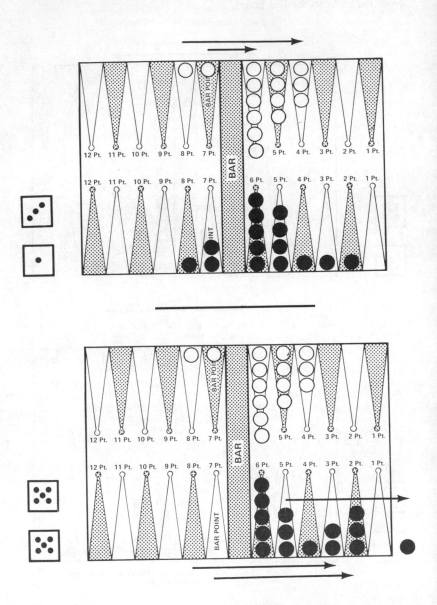

5-5
Three men come in and I can bear a man off the five point putting myself ahead in the race by over twenty pips . . . yummy.

6-4

The six covers the two point and the four covers the three point.

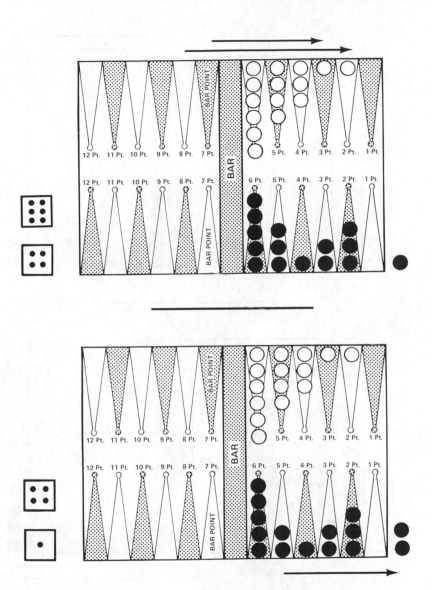

4-1

A man off the four and I'll move the one from the five point to the four point so that I won't miss on fours later.

6-5

Two men off the board.

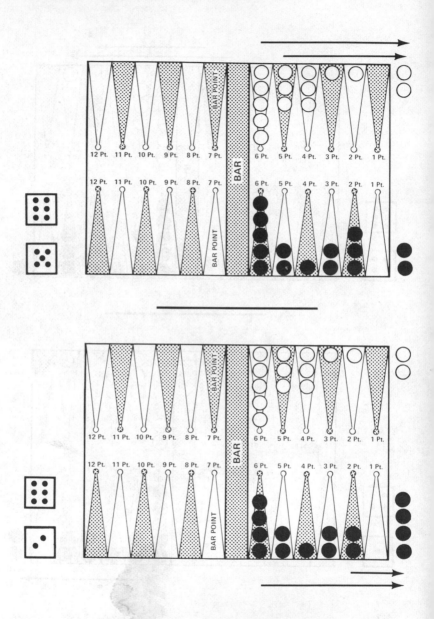

6-2

Two men off the board.

5-1

So many sixes to play . . . I'll take a six off the board using the entire roll.

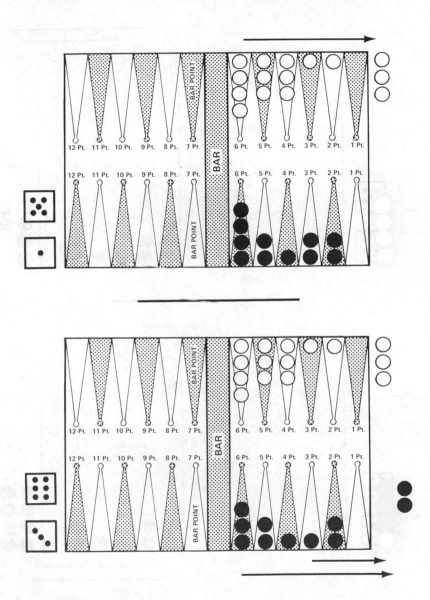

6-3

Two off the board.

5-4
Two men off the board.

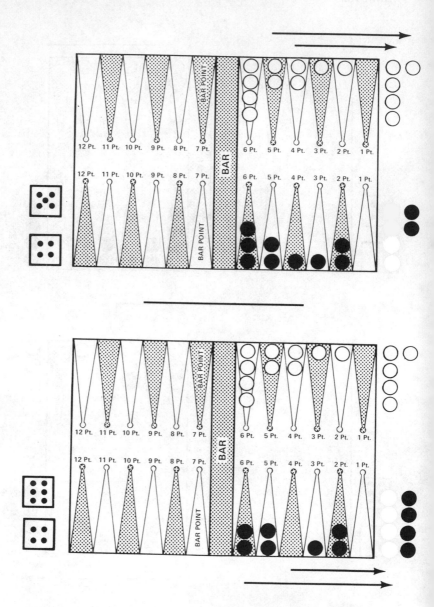

6-4
Two men off the board.

4-3
Two men off the board.

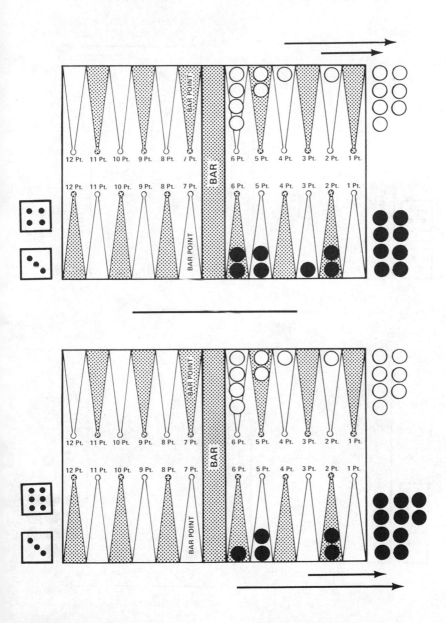

6-3
Two men off the board.

5-2
Two men off the board.

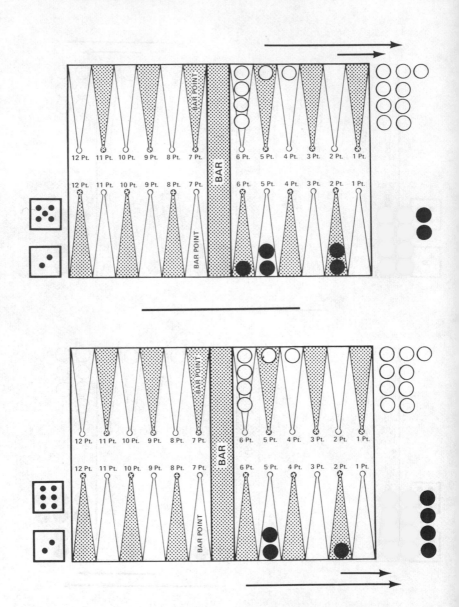

6-2
Two men off the board.

5-4
Two men off the board.

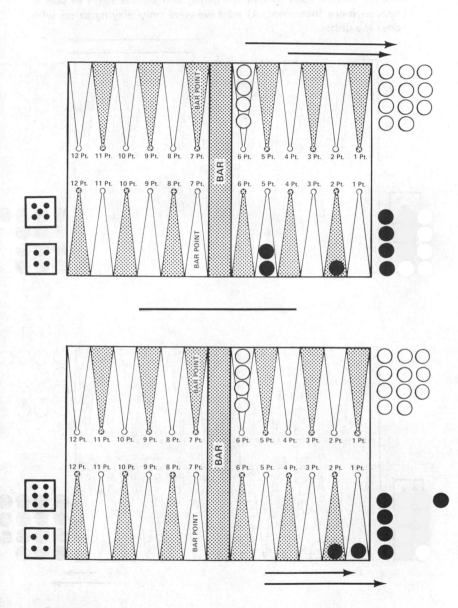

6-4
Since six is *greater* than five, the five comes off the board and four is played from the five to the one point.

3-3

Good, not good enough. Since Sara will be off on her next roll, I needed double sixes to win the game, and believe me, I've seen it happen more than once. At least we were only playing to see who does the dishes.

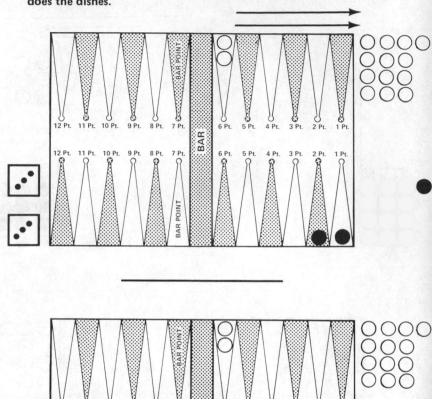

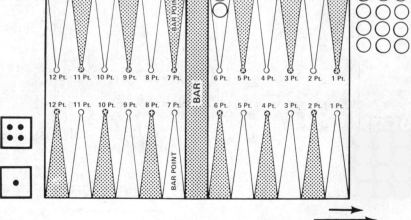

4-1
Gets me off — without dishpan hands.

Fasten your seat belts! You are about to embark on a challenging trip through the imaginative, logical and aggressive approach to backgammon.

In the following game, experts demonstrate a high level of skill and strategy needed to overcome the luck element.

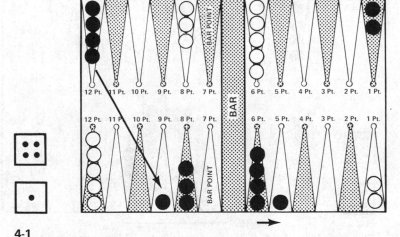

4-1
The four plays from Lee's twelve point to my nine point, a good builder. Rather than split my back men, I chose to slot my five point. This gives me two blots, but only one roll out of 36 would get both.

I wish that I had hit, but I was less than even money to do so. Standard play, I'll bring two builders into my outer board, preparing to make a point soon.

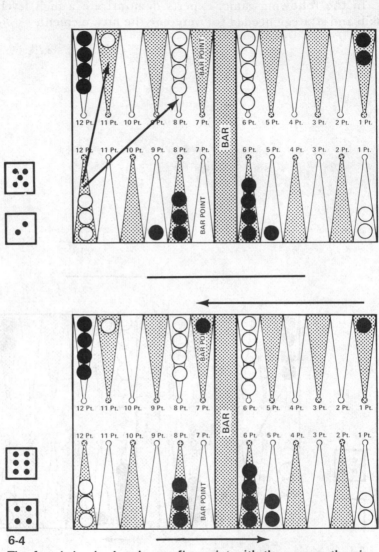

6-4

The four is lovely, I make my five point with the man on the nine point. The six has an option. Although slotting my bar is good and is hit only by sixes, I prefer moving a back man to Lee's bar since I have a point in my board and the return shots, assuming that I am hit, are good.

3-1

I don't want Sara to make my bar so I hit with the one. I like splitting with the three to Sara's four point because of the possibility of being hit on the next roll — if so, the four point is a good landing place for my man.

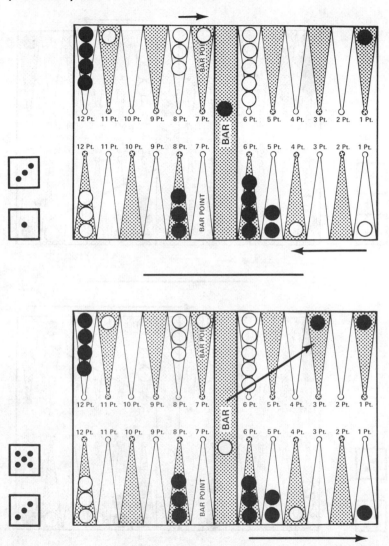

5-3

Not a good number so I want to keep Lee "off balance" by coming in on her three point and hitting on my one point with the five. I plan to get this man back into play later.

3-2

My roll is not so great either and I must employ the same "off balance" tactics by coming in on the two point and hitting on my three point.

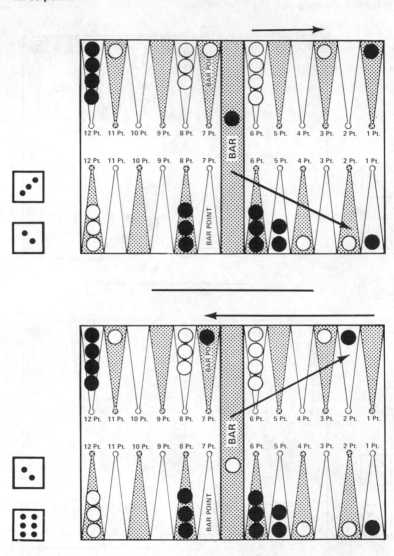

2-6

In with the two, the six I'll take out to Lee's bar rather than expose another man on my own bar.

1-6

Good roll. I come in on the one point, putting Sara on the bar and hit her on my bar with the six, putting a second man on the bar.

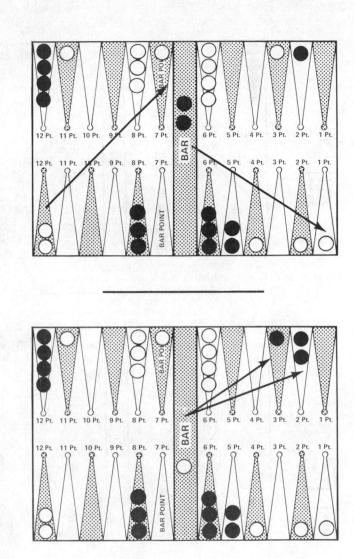

3-2

Both men come in, putting Lee's blot on the three point back where it belongs, on the bar.

6-4

The four makes Sara's four point while the six makes my own bar. This leaves a blot on Sara's twelve point but still seems to be the best play.

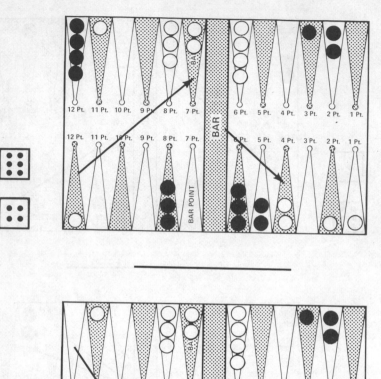

4-4

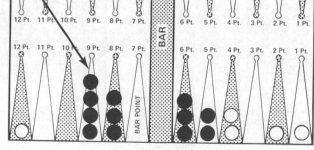

My back men are blocked, leaving me only one good play. I bring all four men from Lee's twelve point to my nine point, which does block Lee's fives from my four point.

6-5

A good defensive play, I make Sara's bar point.

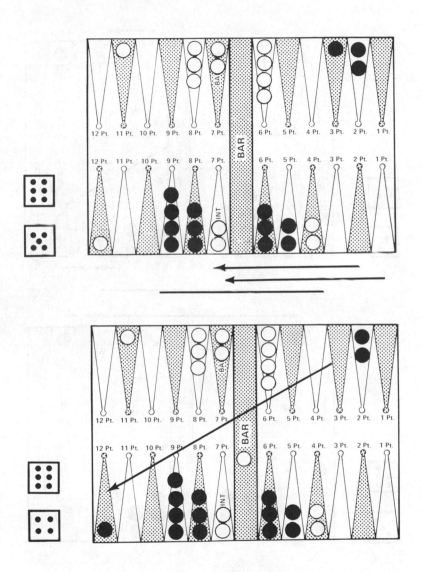

6-4

A well-aimed shot. I hit the blot on my twelve point with the man on Lee's three point.

2-2

One two comes in and moves up to the four point so that it can get out. Two twos make my own four point in an attempt to block the men back.

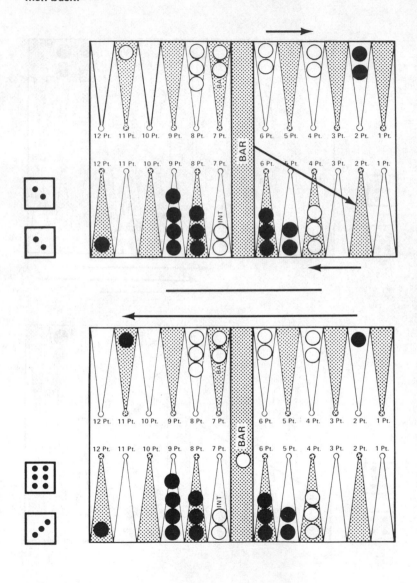

6-3

I can hit the blot on Lee's eleven point.

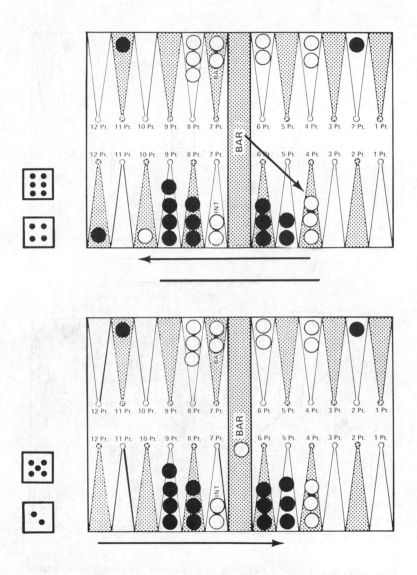

6-4

In and out seems best. Not a great proposition, but the best that I have.

5-2

The two will hit the blot and I will bring the same man in with the five to the five point.

67

3-3

One three brings me on the board. I don't want to leave Sara's bar yet so I will run a man from the four point all the way to my twelve point vulnerable only to direct ones.

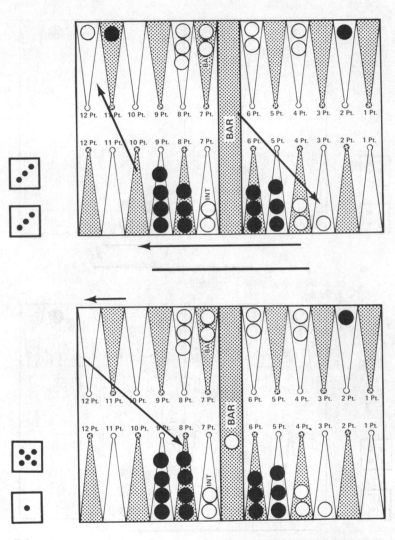

5-1

Two plays to consider. I need the one to move the man on Lee's two point to be able to get out with sixes, but the temptation to hit is too much. I have decided to hit the blot and continue with the same man.

4-3

I bet Sara's sorry that she hit me now. I'll come in on her three point which allows me to vacate the bar with the four. This gives me a pretty good position.

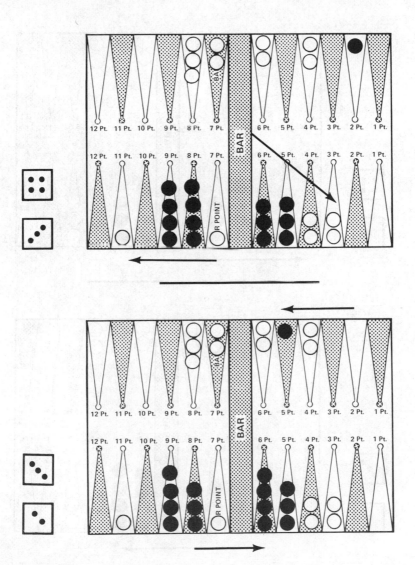

3-2

It's imperative that the three is used to move me to Lee's five point, I don't want to be primed back there. The two just brings a man into my six point.

4-1

Since I can't hit the man on the five point I must leave a trap to get when it leaves my board. I move the man on Sara's bar to her twelve point.

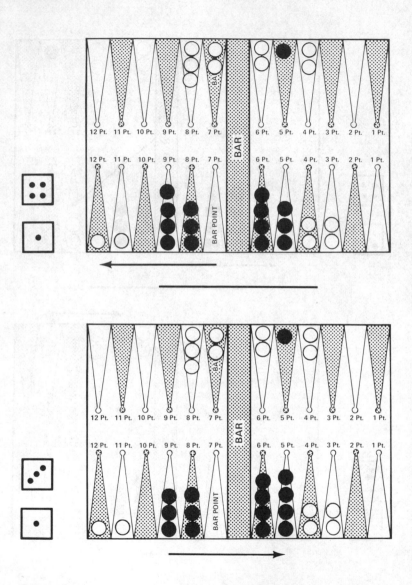

3-1

That used to be a good roll! I'll just bring a man from my nine point to my five point.

6-2

I certainly won't bring a man out of Sara's board to her twelve point
since it's fraught with danger. I want her back behind my prime so
I'll hit with the man on her twelve point.

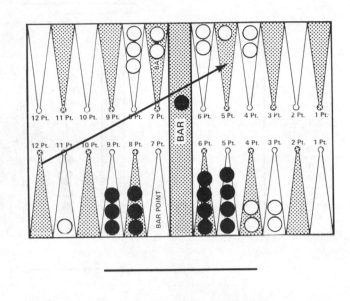

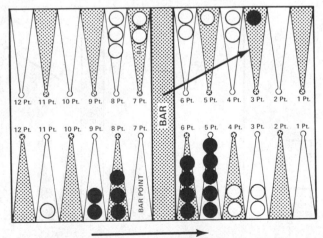

4-3

Three on the board. I don't want to lose a man behind her points so
I'll bring another man into the five point.

4-2

Push her back . . . The two makes my five point, the four hits her again. It won't hurt much if she hits me but it would really smart to have her leave.

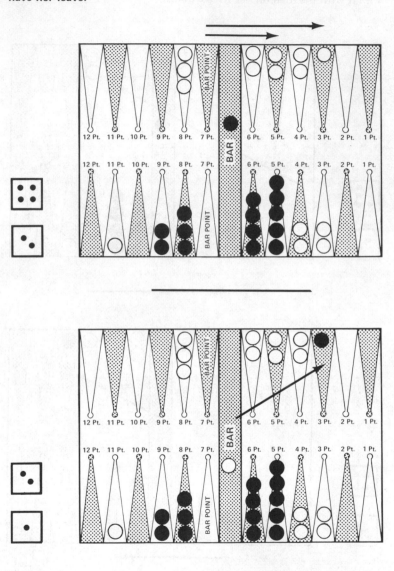

2-1

A hit . . . can't be bad for me.

3-2
On with the two. Because I want more ways to hit again, I bring a
three to my five point.

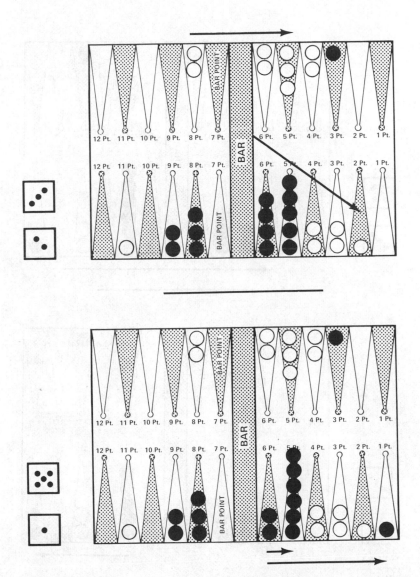

5-1
Yuk! The only playable five moves from my six point to my one
point. The one is also ugly. A man steps from my six to my five
point.

I want out . . . with the man on the two point out to the nine point hoping to catch Sara if she leaves my home before dessert.

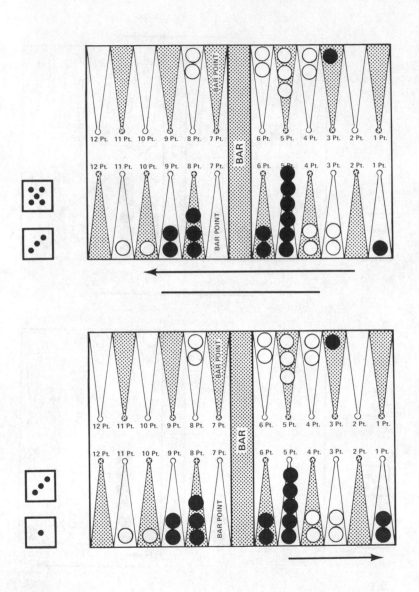

3-1
My one point is ugly, but safe.

74

I could hit her with the man on Sara's eleven point, which is good, but I prefer making my nine point, which is almost as good as a six point prime ... double fours my nightmare.

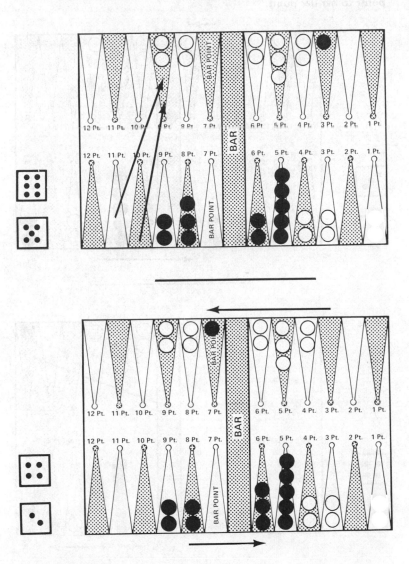

4-2

A desperate escape requires the four to come out to Lee's bar, where I'm hit with ones and twos. The two moves from my eight to six point.

3-1

My game looks good enough to go into a front game and attempt to prime the man, which I place on the bar after a swift hit with the one. The three starts the front game by coming from Sara's four point to her bar point.

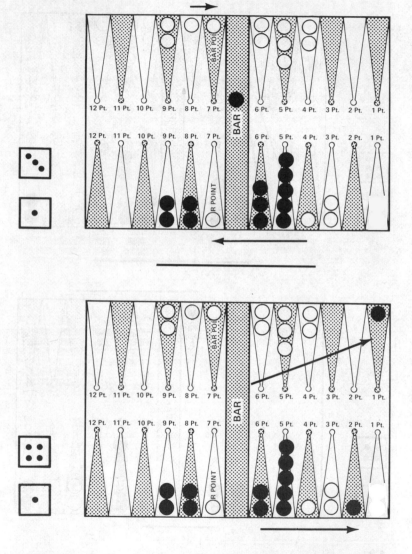

4-1

The one comes on, the only four from the six point to the two point. Help!

3-1

Having both twos and ones to prime her, and a strong position, I would double in money games. But in a match, especially if I were ahead, I might wait another roll. This very good roll makes both bar points.

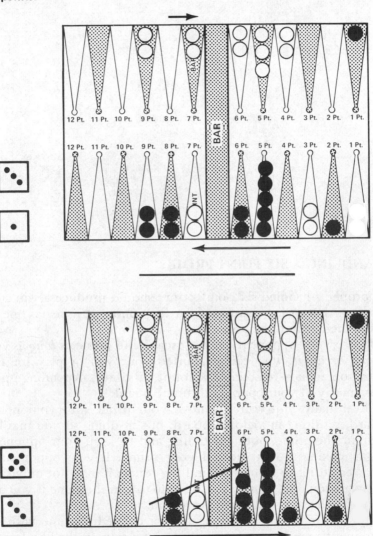

5-3

Disaster strikes, at least I wasn't doubled. The three comes nicely to the six point but I'd like to give away the five. It plays to the four point leaving a direct shot to add to my problems. A good white would double, ending the game.

"A rolling prime gathers no loss."

HANDLING A SIX POINT PRIME:

A properly handled six point prime should produce a win and, in many instances, a gammon for the opponent if he has one or more men behind the prime.

Since your opponent cannot escape the prime *as long as you don't break it,* you can guarantee your win or play for the gammon with a reasonable amount of safety, depending upon the quality of your opponent's home board.

Eventually you want to move your prime into your home board, resulting in a closed board, but in doing so you may hit behind the prime, both for timing and to keep your opponent from making a point behind your prime. If your opponent is allowed to make a point behind the prime, it may not only save the gammon, but he may also be able to win the game if you are forced to leave a shot while bearing in.

In the following position, I have created a prime with an opponent's man on my one point and a man on the bar. I must hit the man on my one point for the two reasons mentioned above. If I am hit, after putting the opponent on the bar, I may even pick up another man, guaranteeing the gammon.

Follow my plays closely and refer to the theories I have described here to comprehend my moves.

78

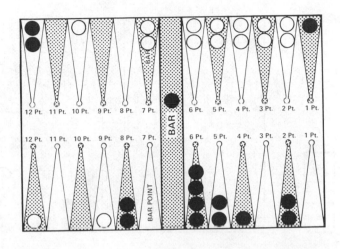

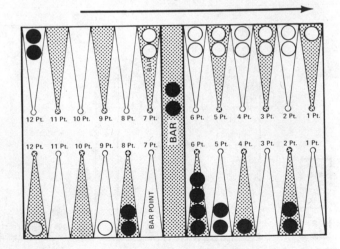

5-4

My man on the ten point hits my opponent on the one point. Only double ones will hurt.

5-1

One hits my blot, the five not playable.

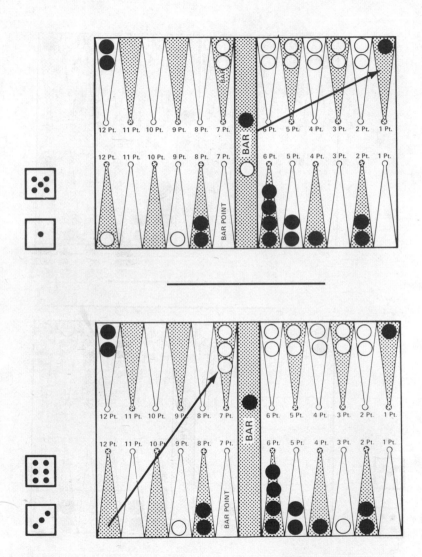

6-3

Three comes on. The six I bring to my bar so that I can continue to hit if necessary.

80

STAY OUT

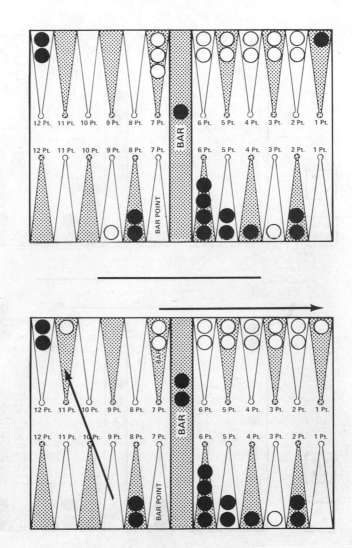

6-5

Hit on the one point again with the man on my bar and bring the man from opponent's nine point to my eleven point.

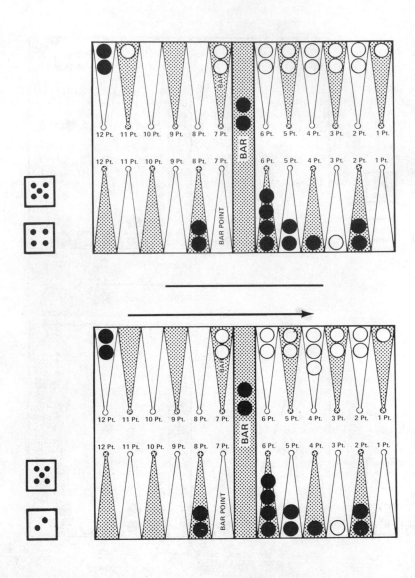

5-2

Although I want to move my trapped man, I can't, so I bring a man into my four point. Double 5's kill me.

4-1
One hits, no four.

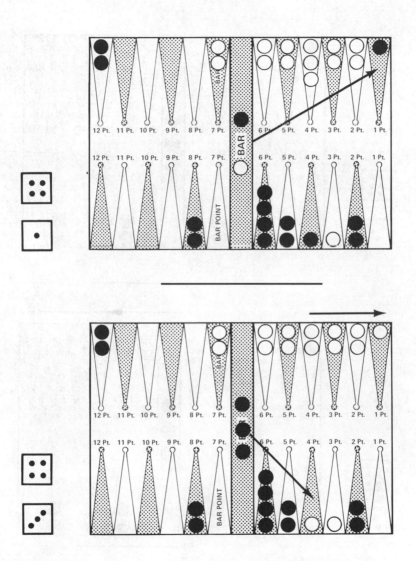

4-3
Four on. I hit again with the three, but am unhappy about losing builders. Three on bar is lovely.

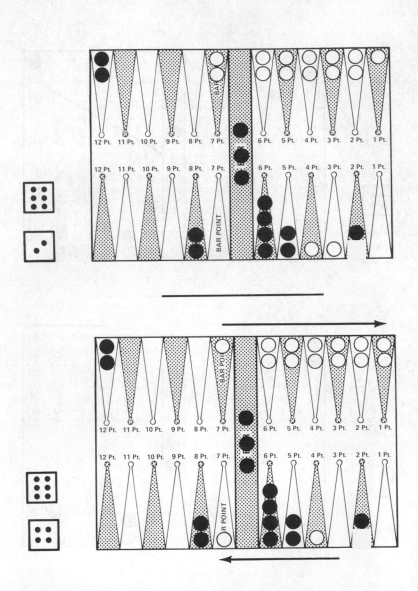

6-4

Time to close board with six. I move a four to the bar so that my
following moves are safe. A gammon is almost assured.

84

"I am the master of my fate, but not the captain of my roll."

CHAPTER IV

UGLY MATHEMATICS

You are about to embark on one of the more tortuous routes on our journey through the thought processes involved in thinking backgammon. Don't despair; all you will need is a little cool for a dispassionate view of this aspect of the game. Numbers aren't scary if you understand them and with a little time and patience you'll be able to see the logic behind them. Since it is so important to understand these principles, go at a pace that is comfortable for you. After a bit of experience, all of these fiendish concepts will settle in your brain and function like the well-oiled parts of a Swiss clock. When your mind begins to feel like an overloaded circuit, don't blow a fuse. Simply put the book down (gently) and reassure yourself that your mind isn't addled.

As any good crap-shooter knows, there are 36 possible rolls on a pair of dice. If you follow this explanation with a pair of dice of unmatched color, you will be able to see why one knows how often certain numbers are rolled.

There are 11 ways to roll a specific number on one die. For example, a 4 will come up on one die with a 4-1, 4-2, 4-3, 4-4, 4-5, and 4-6. Conversely, a 4 will come up on the other die with a 1-4, 2-4, 3-4, 4-4, 5-4, and 6-4. If you have counted, there seem to be 12 ways to roll a 4, but since a double 4 can only be rolled one way, we subtract one roll and come up with 11 ways. Since we know there are 11 ways to roll one number, it follows that there are 22 ways to roll two specific numbers. Right? Wrong. There are only 20 ways to roll, for example, a 4 and a 2 because the 4-2 and 2-4 can't be counted twice. It follows that there are 27 ways to roll three specific numbers, 32 ways to roll four, 35 ways to roll five, and 36 ways to roll all six.

So far we have discussed only the possibilities of rolling a specific number. We must now look at the probabilities of rolling a combination of two numbers of the dice (i.e. 6-3).

Any designated roll of two dice (except for doubles) will occur two times out of a possible 36 combinations. A 6-3, for example, may be rolled as a 6-3 or a 3-6.

Now let's consider why we need know all this mumbo-jumbo. If you are idly sitting on the bar, you may employ your time constructively by figuring out the probabilities of entering your opponent's home board on your next roll. It's easy to see that if your opponent owns only his six point, the only roll that will keep you on the bar is double sixes. Since double sixes will come up only one roll out of 36, the odds that you will enter from the bar are 35 to 1 in your favor. That's an easy one. Table I illustrates the probabilities of entering one man from the bar when your opponent holds one, two, three, four, or five points in his home board. If he holds all six (a closed board), you might employ your time more successfully by thinking about the weather, your latest date or actually working for a living.

TABLE I

PROBABILITIES OF ENTERING ONE MAN FROM THE BAR

Number of points open	Ways to come in	Odds of coming in
5	35	35 to 1 in favor
4	32	8 to 1 in favor
3	27	3 to 1 in favor
2	20	5 to 4 in favor
1	11	25 to 11 against

Table II is an even tougher proposition. You have two men on the bar. You very likely have been doubled. Your acceptance of the double may depend largely upon how many points your opponent holds in his home board and your possibilities of entering with both men on your next roll. If you know your odds it will help you to evaluate your position and impress your opponent at the same time. Remember, a little intimidation goes a long way. By the way, contrary to my readers' general opinion, this table has not been included to intimidate you. In fact, you don't even need to try to assimilate it at this point. I just want you to know that it exists, and when you become more proficient, you may want to use its contents to break your opponent's spirit. Hopefully, he doesn't have the same devious scheme in mind.

TABLE II

PROBABILITIES OF ENTERING TWO MEN FROM THE BAR

Number of points open	Number of men entering	Ways to come in	% of coming in
1	one man in	10	28%
	both men in	1	3%
2	one man in	16	44%
	both men in	4	11%
3	one man in	18	50%
	both men in	9	25%
4	one man in	16	44%
	both men in	16	44%
5	one man in	10	28%
	both men in	25	69%

"How will I hit thee? Let me count the ways."

Since we all leave blots from time to time, it is helpful to know how often they will be hit. Here are two general rules for blot-leavers. (1) *If you leave a blot within range of a direct shot (1←6), the closer you are to your opponent's man, the less likely you are to be hit.* Thus, if you leave a blot one point away from your opponent's man, it will be hit by a one, or 11 times out of every 36 rolls. But, if you leave a blot six points away, it will be hit by any of the following: any 6, 5-1, 1-5, 4-2, 2-4, double three's and double two's; or 17 times out of 36. (2) *If you leave a blot within range of an indirect or combination shot (7→12), the farther away you are from your opponent's man, the less likely you are to be hit* (with one exception). Thus, if you leave a blot seven points or pips away from your opponent's man, it will be hit with a 4-3, 3-4, 5-2, 2-5, 6-1 and 1-6, or six times out of 36 rolls (17 to 1 odds against). When your mind boggles, simply remember "1← 6; 7→12."

Table III illustrates the probabilities of being hit; you may refer to it as often as needed. As in any learning situation, the key is experience and, believe it or not, you will soon be able to quickly calculate the odds in any given position.

TABLE III

PROBABILITY OF HITTING A BLOT

Points away	Ways to be hit	Chances of being hit	Odds against being hit
1	11	31%	25 to 11
2	12	33%	2 to 1
3	14	39%	11 to 7
4	15	42%	7 to 5
5	15	42%	7 to 5
6	17	47%	19 to 17
7	6	17%	5 to 1
8	6	17%	5 to 1
9	5	14%	31 to 5
10	3	8%	11 to 1
11	2	6%	17 to 1
12	3	8%	11 to 1

There are instances where the 1← 6; 7→12 rule does not apply. In Diagram #17, black has left a blot six points away from one of white's men. The blot can only be hit with a six, because white cannot legally move a combination of six (4-2, 5-1, 3-3 and 2-2). The six can be rolled only 11 times out of 36, just as any direct number.

Diagram 17

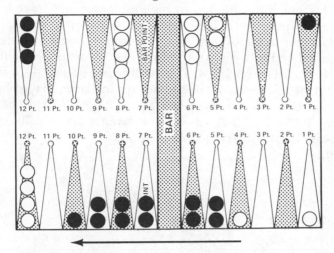

You can learn to play the odds by reducing your chances of being hit. In Diagram #18, black has a one to play. He has left two blots on the board and both are vulnerable to a hit if white rolls a 4 or a 5 (or any combination of those numbers).

Diagram #18

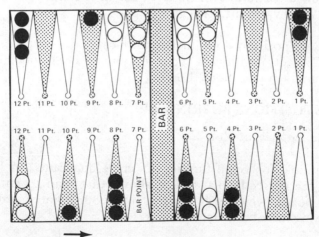

Yet, if you study the position, you will see that black can move his one from his ten to his nine point and leave himself vulnerable only to a four. He has *duplicated* the numbers necessary for a hit by his opponent and decreased his odds in doing so. The blots survive if white is not fortunate enough to roll a four, 3-1, double 2 or (heaven forbid) double 4, or fifteen rolls out of thirty-six. If black had, for instance, played his one from white's nine to white's ten point, he would have been hit by any 5, 3, 2-1, 3-2, or 4-1, or twenty-seven rolls out of thirty-six. What a difference an ace makes!

CHAPTER V

DOWN THE STRETCH

You are almost to the last lap and ready to take a breather. Before you declare victory, it is necessary to learn how to safely bring your men into your home board and bear them off. Please refer to Chapter I for basic rules on bearing off.

Below are a variety of hints to use in the end game position which are divided into two groups:

1) Race position — no further contact
2) Contact position — your opponent holds one or more points in your home board

RACE POSITIONS-BEARING IN:

"Waste not, want not."

1) Look for opportunities to cross quadrants. In Diagram #19, the correctly placed ace allows that man to enter your outer board, which will bring it into your home board with a following roll of a direct six.

Diagram #19

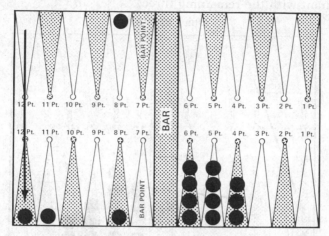

2) In general, bring your men in without "wasting pips." A 6-3 roll in Diagram #20 should be played by moving a man from your twelve point to the six point and a man from the eight point to your five point. If you play it any other way, you come into your home board farther than necessary, which wastes pips.

Diagram #20

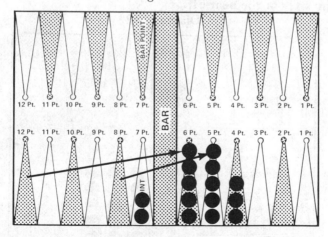

3) Bring as many men as possible into your home board. Contrary to rule two, it is correct to waste a pip or two if it allows you to bring in an extra man as illustrated in Diagram

91

#21. In this case, double threes bring in three men, plus crosses a quadrant with the remaining three.

Diagram #21

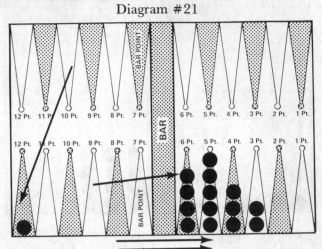

4) Attempt to bear in covering the six, five and four points as equally as possible. This places you in the best possible position to begin bearing off. Diagram #22 shows that position. If you pile all your men on your six point, although you didn't waste pips, you will, in most cases, waste rolls since you require so many sixes in the bear-off.

Diagram #22

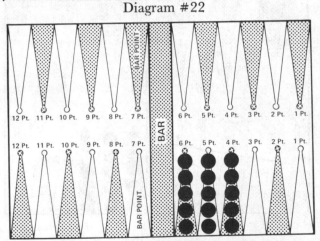

5) If you are in a race and you have to position your men in your outer board, use the same rules as when bearing men off. See "bear off probabilities" described later in this chapter.

RACE POSITIONS-BEARING OFF:

1) When all points in your home board are covered, the dice will designate your play in bearing off. In Diagram #23, a 6-5 roll takes two men off the six point and five point respectively.

Diagram #23

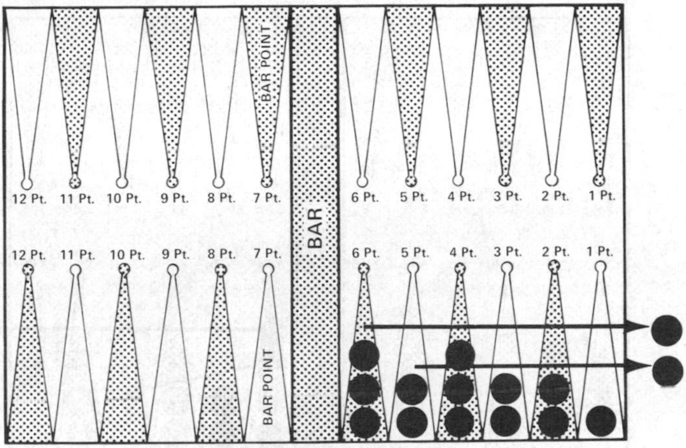

2) If the number rolled is *larger* than your outer man you may convert the number to bear off as illustrated in Diagram #24. A 6-2 is rolled and since six is greater than five, the outer man (the man on the five point) comes off and the man on the two point is borne off naturally.

Diagram #24

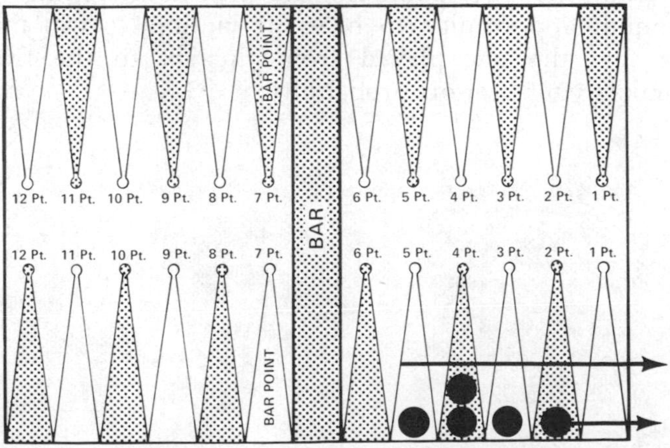

93

3) In Diagram #25, a 6-3 is rolled. The six comes off and the three should be moved from your six point to your three point since it covers another point and minimizes the number of sixes needed to get off.

Diagram #25

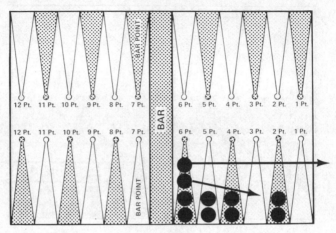

4) In desperate situations when you can count the number of rolls that will get your opponent off, drastic plays are required. In Diagram #26, your opponent is obviously off in three rolls. You must play a 6-1 and you must assume that you will roll double sixes on the following roll. Your best play on that assumption is to bear a man off with the six and move the one from the two point to the one point, giving you the maximum opportunity to bear off in time to win the game. Note that the one played from the six to the five point minimizes your bear-off probability.

Diagram #26

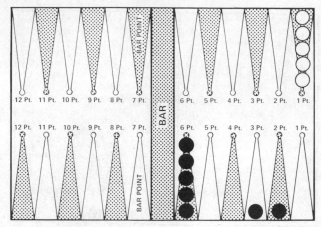

BEAR OFF PROBABILITIES:

To become expert at backgammon you must be able to determine your chances of bearing off two men in any given position. Once you are able to do this, you will find it easier to compute the number of rolls required to bear off three, four or more men. It is particularly important, when a doubling position occurs, to be able to figure the exact probabilities in deciding whether to double or whether to accept a double.

"Bear" with me — it is really not so hard and takes only counting on your fingers and toes. Memorizing these positions saves you brain drain, but if you have the mental tools to figure them out, you won't need that extra initial labor.

The method required in computing a position is to count the number of rolls that will get you off in one roll. Then divide this number by thirty-six, the total number of rolls on a pair of dice, to arrive at the percentage of times you will bear off in one roll in any given position. If you have a tough time at first, I suggest that you use pencil and paper to add up the number of rolls and compute the percentages.

We will start with a few easy positions to compute. In the first position, the simplest method is to work in reverse. By that I mean, as in Diagram #27, only a 2-1 roll prevents a bear off. Since a 2-1 comes up only two times in thirty-six rolls, thirty-four rolls will get you off. Divide thirty-six into thirty-four and you will arrive at the percentage of times you will get off in one roll or in this case 94% . . . that was easy — right?

Diagram #27

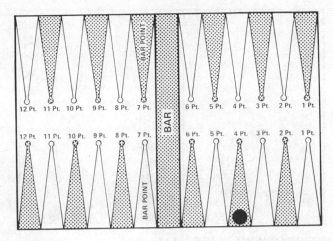

Diagram #28 works the same way. You get your man off in one roll unless you roll 2-1, 3-1 or double aces for a total of five rolls which leaves thirty-one ways to get off for a percentage of 86%.

Diagram #28

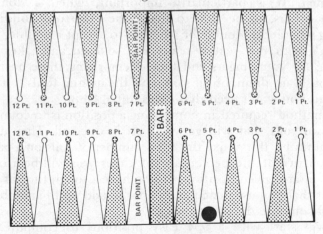

A little rougher, Diagram #29 is a two-man bear-off position. This time you are off unless you roll any number combined with a one — which occurs eleven times out of thirty-six. Therefore, you will get off in twenty-five rolls or 69% of the time.

Diagram #29

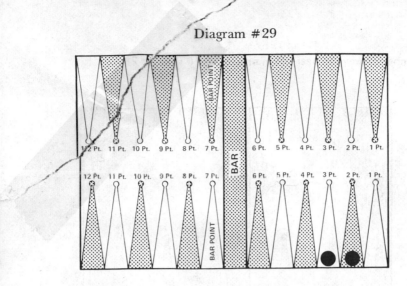

Diagram #30 is typical of one in which you count the rolls that will get you off the board. You are off with 6-5, 6-4, 6-3, 6-2, 5-4, 5-3, 5-2, double sixes, fives, fours, threes and twos for a total of nineteen rolls or 53% of the time.

Diagram #30

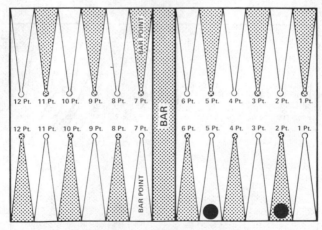

Practice counting the number of rolls required to bear off in Diagrams #31 to #36 until you feel proficient in your calculations. Try to determine the correct answer for each example before reading the explanation below each diagram. A little labor now saves a lot of points later.

Diagram #31

Number of ways to bear off in one roll — 10 rolls or 28%.

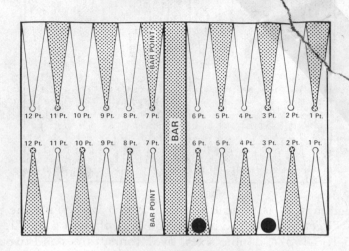

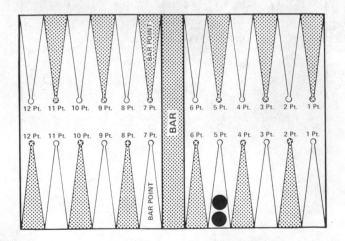

Diagram #32

Number of ways to bear off in one roll — 6 rolls or 17%.

98

Diagram #33

6-1. The six takes a man off and after concentrating on which ace to play, you will find that either move requires 23 rolls to bear off on the next roll, or 64%.

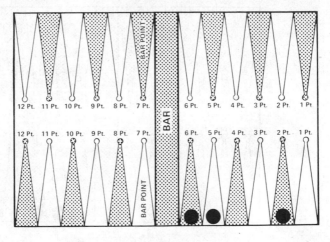

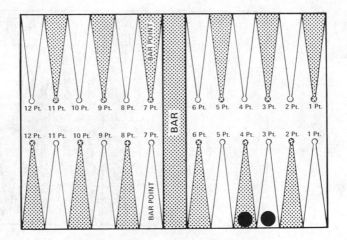

Diagram #34

Number of ways to bear off in one roll — 17 rolls or 47%.

Diagram #35

Number of ways to bear off in one roll — 10 rolls or 28%.

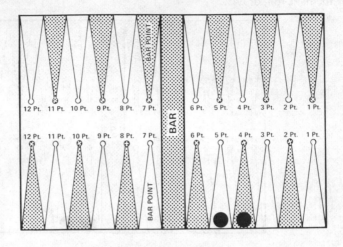

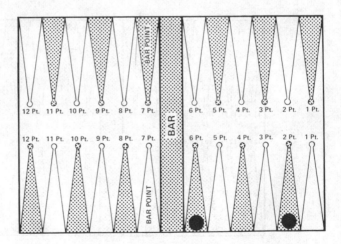

Diagram #36

Number of ways to bear off in one roll — 13 rolls or 36%.

The following are a few general points about bear-off positions for the days you are too tired to figure them out.

1) Men should not be positioned on the same point since less rolls will take them off.

2) When positioning two men, it is never wrong to position one man on the five point and the other one elsewhere. As shown in the following examples, there are less rolls to bear off two men if one is positioned on the five point rather than on other random points.

a) 5-2: less rolls than 4-3 or 6-1
b) 5-1: equal number of rolls as 4-2 and less than 3-3
c) 5-3: less rolls than 4-4 or 6-2
d) 5-4: equal number of rolls as 6-3

3) When a number will not take a man off the board, it will often be played from the six point or from the point that has the most men on it.

4) Consider the number of rolls that it will take your opponent to bear off each time you play your roll.

CONTACT POSITIONS – BEARING OFF:

Your objective in bearing off, when your opponent holds one point or more in your home board, is to attempt to avoid leaving a shot on your roll and prepare to do the same on your following rolls. Sometimes the best played bear-off is rewarded with a direct shot for your opponent, but the law of probabilities should stand behind you most of the time. Don't be discouraged when a disaster occurs and follow these suggestions whenever possible.

1) When bearing in always protect yourself in the event that large doubles may follow on the next roll. The same principle applies in bearing off which usually is protected by staying even on the ends of your home board. Diagrams #37 and #38 show this concept. In #37, you are protected against all numbers. In #38, you have protected against doubles but leave a double shot with 6-5 which leads us to suggestion 2.

Diagram #37

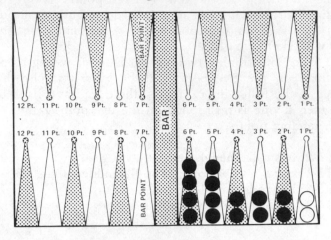

Diagram #38

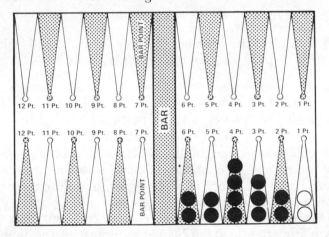

2) Some positions cannot protect against doubles, but it is very important not to leave a double shot. In bearing off, always consider 6-5, 5-4, even 4-3, and more numbers as you become a true expert. In Diagram #39 you roll a 4-1. You can bring the man on the nine point into the four point, which does not leave a shot if you roll double sixes or double fives on the following roll (only two rolls out of thirty-six), or bring it into the five point and move a man from the three point to the two point. This play protects against 6-5 as a double shot and makes 5-4 safe — a much better play.

Diagram #39

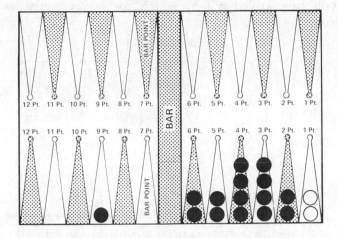

3) Although you must play both numbers if possible, you may play either one first, so if it protects your position, use that option when valid. In Diagram #40, a 6-1 played carelessly would leave a shot, but you can play the ace first from the six point and convert the six to a five to bear it off leaving no shots, thus "burying a number."

Diagram #40

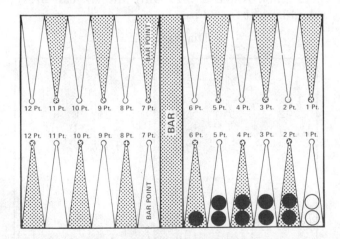

4) When the only way to play both numbers leaves one or more shots, you have no alternative; this is called a forced

roll, as illustrated in Diagram #41. Here, you grimace to find that you have rolled a 6-5, which to play properly leaves a double shot — better luck next time!

Diagram #41

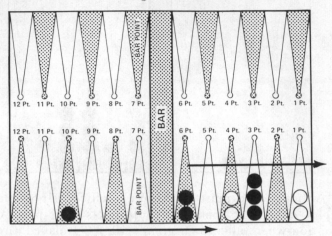

5) In general, break from your outer points when it does not violate another rule, and if you must leave a shot, choose one that if not hit will most likely eliminate future shots.

6) When you can play one of your numbers, but not both, you must play the higher number as sadly illustrated in Diagram #42 where black rolled a 6-2. Only the six can move, which leaves a double shot for white.

Diagram #42

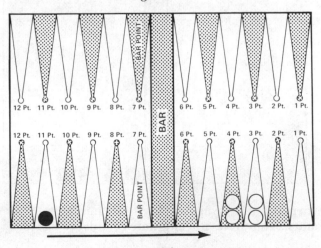

CLOSED BOARD:

Diagram #43 is a perfect closed board, ready to bear men off. When your opponent is on the bar, protect against doubles, usually playing for "even on the end" as mentioned earlier in this chapter. Your opponent may not roll until you open a point in your board.

Diagram #43

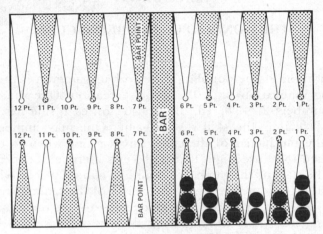

NOTE: A backgammon board can be set up in four different ways: White's home board in the upper left, upper right, lower left, or lower right. The previous diagrams in this book had White's home board in the upper right. From here to the end, the White home board will be in the lower right. (In backgammon, you have to stay on your toes!) Practice playing with White's home board in all four places, so you'll become familiar with the board from every angle. Incidentally, in tournament play the home board is usually on the side closest to the light source.

CHAPTER VI

THE WONDERFUL DOUBLING CUBE

The addition of the doubling cube to backgammon is the most exciting innovation since the game's creation. One square die with numbers 2, 4, 8, 16, 32, and 64 on each side has added many facets to the skill of the game. One may immediately grasp the mechanics of the cube, but learning when to double and when to refuse might take a player a lifetime of experience.

At the start of the game, the doubling cube is placed with the numeral sixty-four face up in the center of the table. It remains in this position until one player decides to use the cube. The cube is used when either player decides he has a sufficient advantage in the game. Prior to your turn to roll, you may pick up the cube, turn it to the numeral two, and move it to your opponent's side of the table. You then wait, before you roll, to allow your opponent to decide what to do. He may take the cube, place it in front of him, say, "I accept the double," and play now at two units rather than one. Or, if he agrees that you have a considerable edge in the game, he may decide not to continue playing and thus give up one unit. In that case the game would end, you would start over, and the person who doubled would be plus one.

I think the above situation is somewhat similar to a poker game in which you are looking at a very good hand and you want to increase the stake of your game. You raise your bet and your opponent has the same option. He may meet your bet and continue to play the hand or he may fold. In poker, however, you do not see your opponent's position, whereas in backgammon, you can both look at the same position and evaluate it. This is one of the most unique aspects of the game because two players, looking at exactly the same position, may come up with opposite conclusions.

One's knowledge of the technical aspect of a position is of key importance in evaluating a game, but one's objectivity and emotional condition is also very important. Here, psychology plays a very large part in the use of the doubling cube. Let's say that you have doubled the cube to two and your opponent has accepted the double, placing the cube on his side of the table face up. A few rolls later, his position improves sufficiently to give him the better position. He may then take the cube, which is now at two, turn it to four, and give it back to you. You then have the same options as your opponent had before. You may accept the game at four and play for four units or you may drop it, losing two points to your opponent. Hypothetically, this operation could go on from two to four to sixty-four, and I have even heard of games where the cube has reached 256. But in reality, although it's very exciting, it is not good backgammon and I doubt that it would occur when both players have been correctly using the cube.

Automatic Doubles

Automatic doubles occur when on the very first roll of the game both players roll the same number. They do not occur in backgammon tournaments and they have no proper place in the game, but are frequently used among players playing for money. I do suggest, though, that you allow only one automatic double, which would start the cube at two. It is not good practice to allow more than one, in which case you might even start a game with the cube at eight or sixteen which is a very expensive and unnecessary proposition. I would be wary of an opponent who encouraged you to use unlimited automatic doubles. His psychology is that, since he feels he is a better player, he wants more money involved in the game. It is not good practice to play against such tactics.

Timing the Double

The timing in the use of the doubling cube is extremely important because too often you will be in a position in which you consider a double, decide to wait one more roll, and find that in that one roll your opponent's position improved sufficiently so that you could no longer double. It takes a great

107

deal of judgment to know when to double. In starting to use the doubling cube, I suggest that as soon as the game commences, prior to every roll, you ask yourself, do I have a double? This method of self-discipline will keep you constantly aware that you might want to double, and you will at least not have lost the position or the power of doubling through lack of thought. You must realize that when you double and your opponent accepts, he gains possession of the doubling cube and may later have the opportunity to redouble you, in which case you would have to make a decision at the four level. Because owning the cube allows you to finish the game, you must be especially careful about redoubling your opponent, thereby giving up possession of the cube. I have often seen a situation where a player has been caught in the momentum or the excitement of the game and doubled prematurely. A good example is when you have a poor position but your opponent rolls while on the bar and doesn't come in. Your actual position is no stronger than it was the prior roll but now you double (thinking you've just gained an edge) without evaluating the relative strength of your position in the game. I think, basically, you are caught in the momentum of that roll and have made an error in your judgment, so it is always important to take that extra second to evaluate each position. One suggestion you may follow as a general rule in a contact position is that it is not good to double until you have made at least one point in your inner board. There are exceptions to this, but at the beginning this will help you to learn when to double.

Counting the Race

There will be many times in the course of your backgammon career when you will be involved in simple race positions with no possibility of contact. If there is a large discrepancy in pip count, you will be able to visually evaluate your chances of winning or losing the game and doubling or taking a double. But there are also many close races and you must be able to count your position and your opponent's position to find out where you stand.

In Diagram #44, both players have all their men in their home boards and are ready to bear them off.

108

Diagram #44

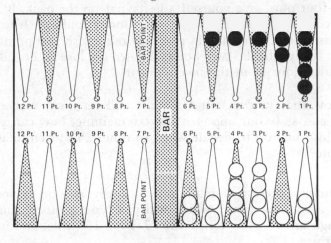

It is black's roll and he would like to know if he has a large enough lead to double white. He does not want to give white a chance to roll a large set of doubles to win the game. If black has a large enough lead, white should pass and give black one point in the score. To determine the count, black proceeds to multiply the number of men on each point by the number of the point. If you read the discussion while looking at the diagram, you will be able to easily understand the count. Since black has five men on his one point, he multiplies five times one and totals a five pip count for the one point. With three men on the two point, he multiplies three times two and totals a six pip count for the two point. With two men on the three point, he multiplies two times three and totals a six pip count for the three point. With two men on the four point, he multiplies two times four and totals an eight pip count for the four point. With two men on the five point, he multiplies two times five and totals a ten pip count for the five point. With one man on the six point, he multiplies one times six and totals a six pip count for the six point. Black adds the pip count of the six points and his position totals a pip count of forty-one. Black's count is meaningless until he counts white's pips to determine the difference between the two positions.

Count white's position on your own. If you total a count of fifty-four pips, give yourself a hefty pat on the back. Black has a thirteen pip lead in the race and should double. White, unless he has loaded dice, should pass and relinquish one point rather than the probable two points he would lose if he takes the double. More about this in a moment.

Now that you've found a quick and easy way to count the pips you and your opponent have remaining, how can you use this information to decide when to double or when to accept a double?

Luckily, there is a simple rule to apply as soon as you enter into a running game, which will give you a quick and close-enough answer. It's called the "7 1/2 - 15" rule, and it works like this:

1. Count your total number of remaining pips.
2. Count your opponent's total number of remaining pips.
3. Find the difference, which is the lead you or your opponent has.

If you're ahead, should you double? To find out, divide your lead by your pips. If your lead is at least 7 1/2% or higher than your pips, double.

For example, if you have 100 pips and your opponent has 90, your lead is 10% of your pips. Double.

If you're behind, and your opponent doubles, should you accept? To find out, divide his lead by *his* pips. If his lead is 15% of his pips or less, accept.

In the case above, you should double, and your opponent should accept.

This "7½-15" rule is perfect unless you've reached the level of expert, in which case you'll want something a little more accurate.

Table IV is the best thing worked out so far to determine whether you should double, or accept a double. In order to double your opponent, you should have at least a 63% chance to win, and in order to take a double, you should be no more than a 24% underdog.

TABLE IV

RACE DOUBLES AND TAKES
(with doubling cube in the middle)

Pips ahead in the race	0	4	8	12	16	20
Pips remaining in my count						
60	62%	67%	77%	83%	87%	92%
70	61%	66%	75%	81%	86%	90%
80	59%	65%	73%	80%	84%	88%
90	58%	64%	71%	78%	82%	86%
100	58%	63%	70%	76%	80%	84%
110	57%	62%	69%	75%	79%	83%

The count may be simplified by using a method called the "cross-count." In Diagram #45, black may count the positional difference by subtracting and adding the difference of each point.

Diagram #45

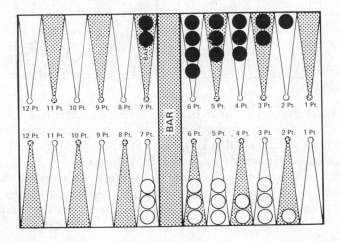

111

Since black has one less man on the bar or seven point, he is ahead seven pips. With one more man on the six point, he loses six pips and now has a total lead of one pip. Since black and white have an equal number of men on the five point, the count remains the same. Black loses four more pips on the four point, and is now down three. He gains three pips on the three point, and is now even. The position is equal on the two point, and we arrive at no pip difference in the positions.

When both players have their men on the one, two and three points, the pip count becomes irrelevant. Since both players will be able to bear off a minimum of two men on every roll, the race position is determined by counting the number of remaining rolls, rather than pips.

In Diagram #46, black has ten men left to bear off and white has twelve.

Diagram #46

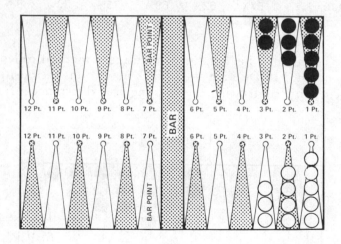

Since black figures to bear off two men on each roll, he will be off in five rolls and white will be off in six (providing neither player rolls doubles). Black is, therefore, one roll ahead in the race with a maximum of six rolls left in the game.

If you each have six rolls or less remaining in the game and all the men are on the one and two points, you should double. Your opponent should take with at least five rolls remaining in the game. With four rolls or less, he should fold the double.

112

When your opponent has put one of your men on the bar, has a closed board, no men off and doubles, your ability to accept depends upon the number of men you have taken off your own home board. Table V illustrates what percent chance you have of winning the game based on the number of men off your board.

TABLE V

Chance of winning when your opponent has hit your blot and closed his board. (A take of the double is correct with 5 men off your board.)

Four men off . . . . 17% chance to win

Five men off . . . . 26% chance to win

Six men off . . . . 32% chance to win

Seven men off . . . . 41% chance to win

Eight men off . . . . 56% chance to win

Nine men off . . . . 64% chance to win

Ten men off . . . . 71% chance to win

Eleven men off. . . . . 80% chance to win

If you have two men on the bar, pass all doubles and cry.

In a race position, there is a limited chance of being gammoned (in which case you would lose twice the stake), so you might often take a double hoping to roll doubles to catch up in the race. However, you must remember that your opponent has equal opportunity to roll doubles and win the game.

A position that involves contact is more difficult to evaluate, but I have a few keys to help you in deciding whether or not to take a double. Your first consideration is, do you think you can be gammoned in this game? If so, you should not take the double, since the liability is too great. A take is based on a three to one mathematical probability. In other words, in evaluating the position, if you were to play this same game four times and

113

you could expect to win the game one time, then you may take the double as long as it is not a gammon position. If you are doubled in this game and you fold each time, you will lose four points for a score of minus four. If you take the double all four times and win only once, you lose six points and win two points, which is the same as if you had dropped all four games. Your score would still be minus four. Therefore, in taking this game, you have not increased your minus expectation. In fact, by possessing the cube, you may increase your plus expectation by winning a game at a higher level or winning a gammon or backgammon.

Another clue in taking a double is that when you hold your opponent's five point, or even his four point, it is a position in which it will be very difficult for your opponent to prime you. So, in many of these games you will have a chance to get a shot at your opponent and possibly win the game. Although this rule does not always apply, the five or four point should give you consideration for a take.

Although doubles and takes are very controversial, even among experts, I have created several samples of positions in which one player would double and his opponent may take or reject the double. I suggest that you set up these positions on your own board and study the explanations I have presented.

Diagram #47   White Doubles

Lee:

Black: "I don't like it since white may make the 5 pt. priming me, or point on me the very next roll. Also, my men are advanced and my board may break." Pass.

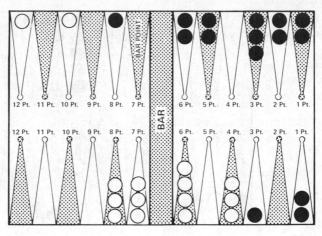

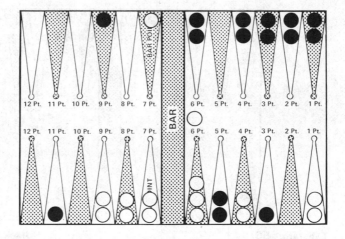

Diagram #48   Black Doubles

Sara:

White: "Much too gammonish because I'm likely to have two on the bar while black has a five point board. I definitely want out." Pass.

115

Diagram #49   White Doubles

Lee:

Black: "Debatable, but although white may hit two of my men, this roll, my board is pretty good and he doesn't have his 5 pt. or his bar. I'll take this one."

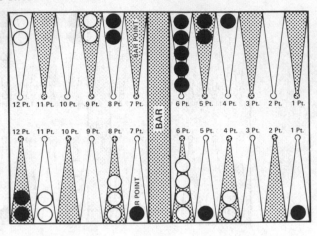

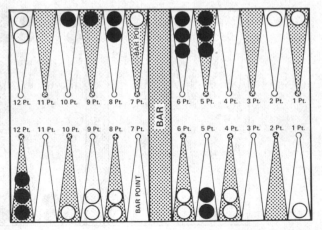

Diagram #50   Black Doubles

Sara:

White: "I'm not fond of the blot on my 1 pt. which gives black so much freedom to double hit me, but if I can make black's 3 or 4 pt., my game should be playable. I'll take, and hope he can't make his bar."

116

Diagram #51

Lee:

Black Doubles

White: "Yuk! Facing a five point prime, or worse, in addition to my extra blot on the 12 pt. I pass, quickly."

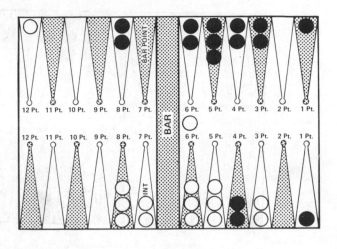

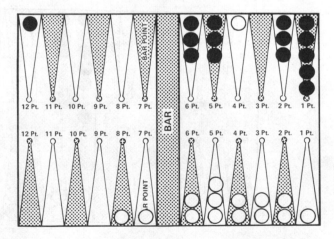

Diagram #52

Sara:

Black Doubles

White: "No gammon here but at best I'm behind in the race and because black can hit and run with small numbers and come in with large ones safely, I don't figure to get a shot. Pass."

117

Diagram #53   Black Doubles

White: "Black may make his 8 pt. or his bar but he will need to get his men past my 4 pt. prime — not so easy. A take for sure."

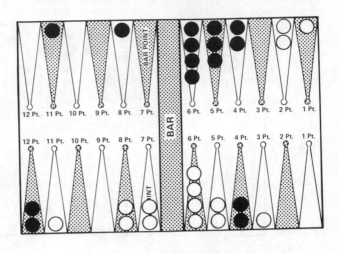

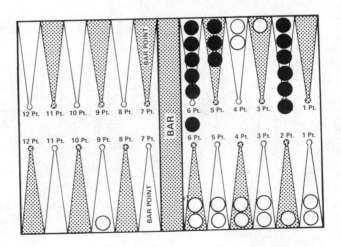

Diagram #54   White Doubles

Black: "Sevens close me out and ones pick up the blot on the two pt. I'd take without the man on the nine pt. but a pass seems safer."

Diagram #55   Black Doubles

White: "Worse than #53, black has made his bar and may make either his 8 pt. or his 3 pt. This time, I pass."

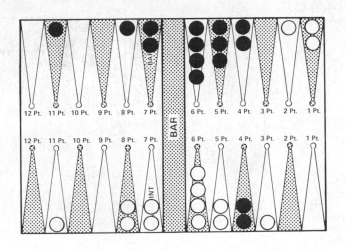

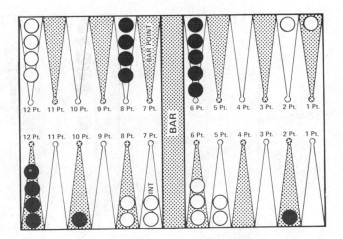

Diagram #56   White Doubles

Black: "I'm primed on white's 2 point and my men look like shishkebabs. Pass this one."

Diagram #57   Black Doubles

White: "I'm on the bar but the 4 pt. gives me safety and if I enter on
the two, better yet, take."

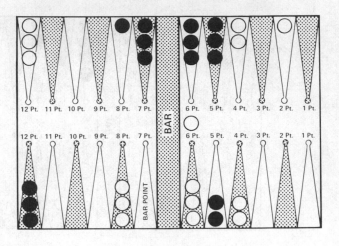

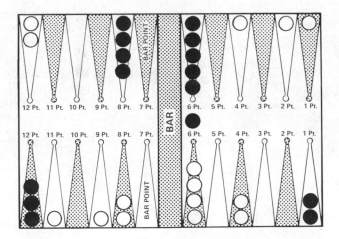

Diagram #58   White Doubles

Black: "Not that it couldn't change, but I don't like positions
without points, rather than try a new game, pass."

120

The most difficult problem is when you are doubled in a back game position. (See Chapter VII: "The Back Game.") You must immediately consider the probability that when playing a back game, if you don't win, you may be gammoned. Because of the likelihood of being gammoned, in order to take the double, you must feel assured of your ability at timing the back game. In tournaments, it is usually not advisable to take a double in a back game, because to lose four points in a short match is enough to put you considerably behind. However, in head-to-head play (that's a non-tournament contest), I am more inclined to take a double with a well-timed back game.

PSYCHOLOGY AND PLOYS:

Becoming a winner involves a great deal more than mastering the technical aspects of the game of backgammon. Understanding your opponents' habits, and overcoming your own bad ones, are prime ingredients in winning and enjoying the game. The doubling cube best illustrates this point. When you arrive at a position which requires making a decision about whether to double, you must consider several facts before giving up the cube to your opponent. Generally, his mental state and his habits are important considerations as well as the mathematical and technical judgment of the game. Psychological evaluation of the setting adds a challenging aspect to the goal of winning. Winning is your goal, but making your opponent comfortable with his loss is very important if you wish to play him again. A defeated player probably will not play you if he is humiliated or convinced that he is a sure loser. Your best etiquette must always be displayed. You should play and act in good taste at all times. Personally, I find mastering my own emotions and ego the greatest challenge and also the most rewarding in terms of my own growth and self-discipline.

Handling Lady Luck

When luck is turning favorably for your opponent your emotional fortitude is put to the test. Don't gripe about his good rolls. Eventually yours will come. It is always well to comment "good luck" or "nicely played." If I have rolled a very bad number, rather than grimace and groan, I try to

121

cheerfully play it as quickly as possible, especially in the situation that if I give added time and attention to the play my opponent will double me.

Tempo in such situations will keep the cube away until you are able to improve your position enough to happily take it. In desperate situations, sometimes a quick hit, which puts your opponent on the bar, even if you are leaving blots in your inner board, will prevent the cube from coming your way. Your positive attitude has to affect him. Your body position exhibits your aggressive interest in the game. I like nothing better than to see my opponent sitting with his head in hand debating his problem or slouching as if too tired to think.

Then there are the days when you lead a charmed life. Every time you roll, a lovely number comes up. You are going to win, probably even when you are not at your best. Don't be a "chirper." He is hurting enough with your good luck. I would rather have him feel that I was very lucky that day than feel he has been outplayed so badly that he doesn't wish to return.

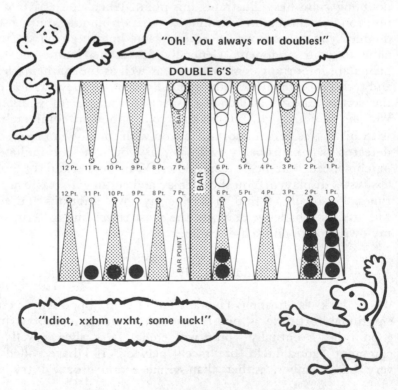

"To hit or not to hit, that is the question."

CHAPTER VII

THE BACK GAME

Remember those games when every blot you left was hit, putting you well behind in the race? The remedy for that malady is the back game which, pardon the chauvinistic phrase, separates the men from the boys.

When you master the back game and can aggressively play without fear, you are an expert. Bad luck over a losing position can be converted to a challenging win.

Praise enough for the lordly back game. Now let's find out how to win a back game. In general, the back game begins when you have made at least two points in your opponent's home board. Your goal, once you hold these points, is to build your own inner board so that when your opponent attempts to bear in, leaving you a shot, your inner board is strong enough to win the game if you hit his blot. The secret to success, therefore, is *timing*—a deceptively simple concept, but the crux of the game.

The matter of which points to hold has been battered around among experts without total agreement, but generally holding the one and three points is preferred. Holding the one and two points is also very popular because your opponent cannot play behind you as easily. Although playable, I've had much less success with the one and four point game, one and five point game, two and five point game, and even less with the four and five point game since my opponent jumps over my trap easily — some trap!

I have been told that in back games you win or get gammoned. The latter occurs more when your timing is too fast and you are forced to leave with your front man. See Diagram #59. White rolls a 6-1.

Diagram #59

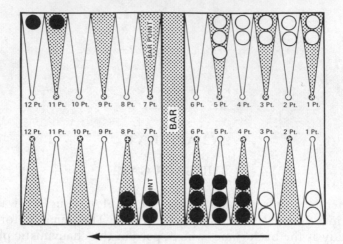

Here, white must run with a man from his opponent's three point. This allows black to point on his three point and possibly pick up the blot on his ten point which puts two men on the bar. As a result, white is likely to be gammoned.

Although the gammon threat is there, better technique lessens the possibility. Even so, I'm less inclined to play back games in a tournament, giving due respect to my advisors.

To begin to understand the concept of timing, follow our sample game closely. When your timing is "too fast," an unnecessary blot is left not out of "chutzpah," but of necessity to correct timing.

4—1: Being an aggressive player, I slot my five points with the one and bring a builder from Sara's 12 point to my own nine point. I'll only be hit 15 times out of 36 and if I'm not, I'll be a big favorite to make my valuable five point.

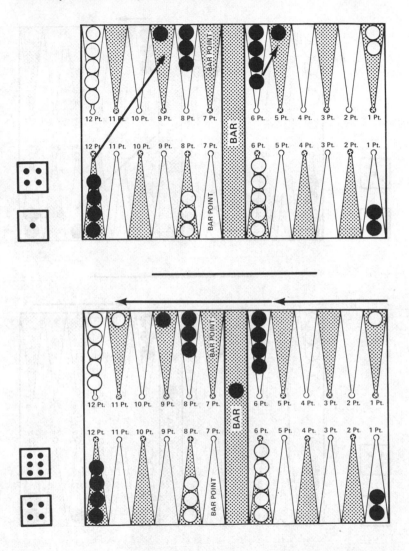

6—4: Certainly, I will hit Lee's blot on her five point, and for lack of a better play, I will continue to her eleven point with the same man. The blot is only exposed to twos and Lee is on the bar.

125

3—1: Because I still want to make my five point, I will enter Sara's board on her three point and slot my five point again . . . better luck next time.

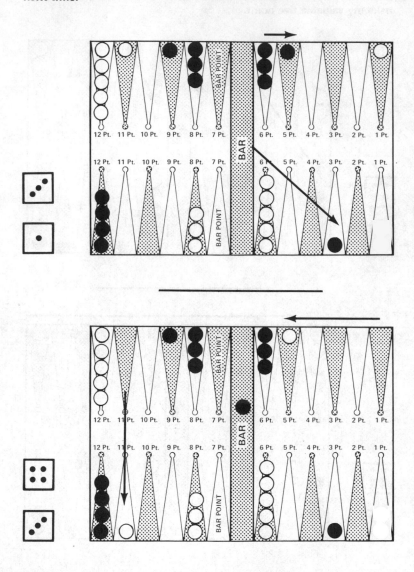

4—3: Good shot. I will hit the blot on the five point with my four and bring my blot to my own eleven point which is an excellent builder for me.

3–2: So far my aggressive moves have been punished. Behind in the race, I must continue with a blot-hitting contest until the smoke clears. Therefore, I enter Sara's board with the two and hit her blot on my five point with my three.

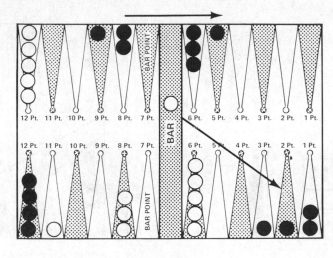

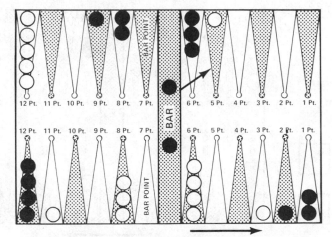

5–3: Lee is beginning a back game and my best defense now is to attempt to keep her from making a second point in my board. I will hit her man on the five point and also hit her man on my three point. Two on the bar can't be bad, and her board is not dangerous for me if I'm hit.

4–2: From the bar, my men enter on the two and four points.

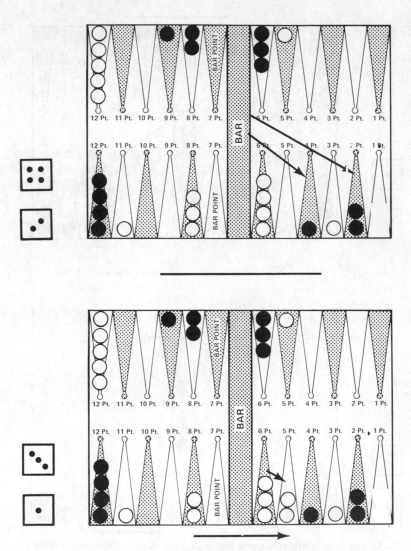

3–1: Although the three could be used to cover my man on the three point, I must resist the temptation and make my own five point. Lee is in a back game and hitting my man would not help her with no points in her own board.

3-2: Now in a back game, I'm not afraid to leave blots. They will, in fact, help me with my timing. So, I'll hit Sara's man on the five point with my three and play the two from Sara's two point to her four point which will give me a modicum of safety. If I am able to make three points in her board, it will be very difficult for her to bear in without leaving a shot for me.

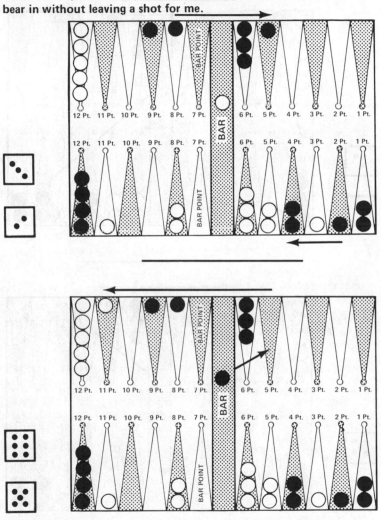

6-5: Wish I didn't have to hit her but the five leaves me no choice. The six I will use taking the same man to Lee's eleven point.

2—2: One two brings me on the board, making Sara's two point. Still happy to be hit some more, I use my man on my nine point to hit the blot on the five point. I'll utilize my last two by bringing a builder from Sara's twelve point to my eleven point.

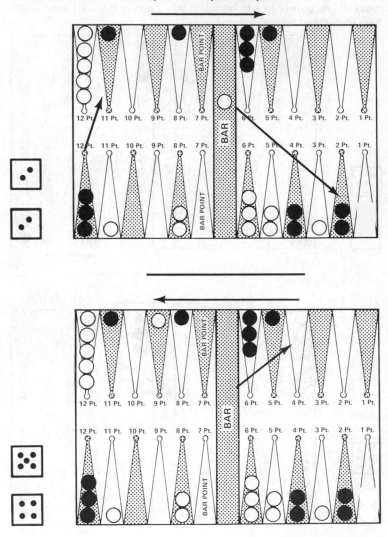

5—4: I won't oblige Lee by hitting her anymore. I come in on her four point and move with the same man to her eight point.

5—4: Live by the gun . . . I'll hit Sara on my eight point with a man on her twelve point and continue by slotting it on my four point. She may be forced to hit with this pseudo-masochistic play.

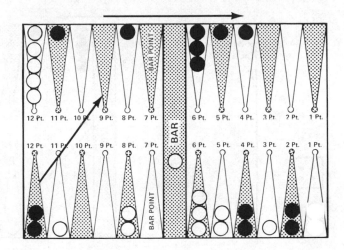

6—5: If she thinks I'll give her two more men back, she doesn't know how I hate violence. I have to hit her on the five point but the six I'll use to slot my own bar. Making my bar would give me a four point prime and if she comes in and hits me there, I would welcome that too.

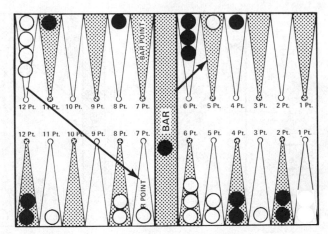

4—3: Coming in on the four point and I'll hit again on my five point.

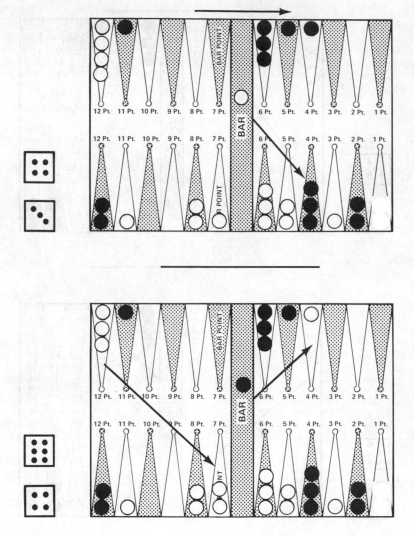

6—4: Another unavoidable hit on her four point. I can make my bar with the six.

4–3: My four on again since I don't wish to slow Sara down by hitting her blot. I'll slide my three from my eleven point to my eight point.

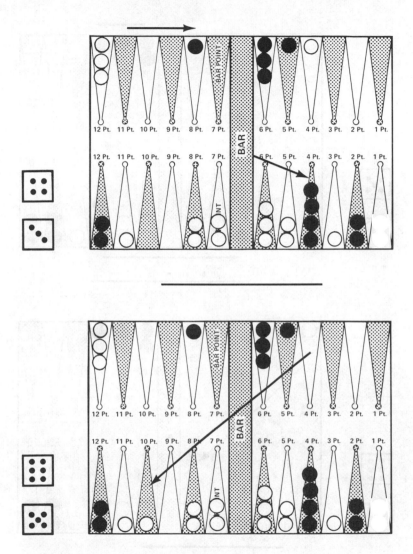

6–5: All the way with my man on Lee's four point bringing it to my ten point.

5—2: Since hitting Sara would slow her down, I move a man from her four point to her nine point and slot my four point with the two. I am preparing to build my own board.

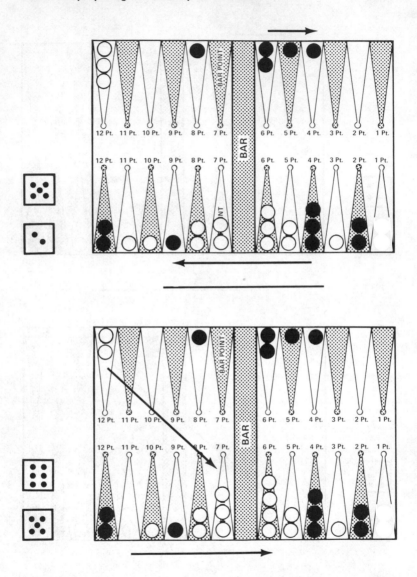

6—5: My six moves to my bar, an excellent builder. Because I would like to make my ten point to block Lee's sixes, I will leave my man there and play the five into my six point.

2–1: Choices. I could make my five point but can probably do it next roll. Instead I move my man on Sara's nine point to her twelve point so that I will have an extra man for my board.

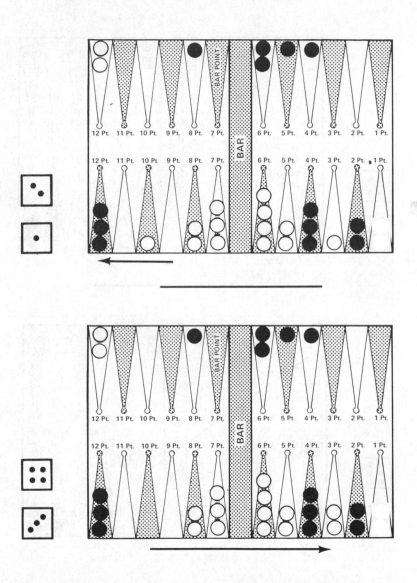

4–3: Time to cover my blot on the three point with the three and pick up the blot on the ten point, bringing that man in.

135

5—3: Sara is getting close to bringing her men in so it's important to clean up my board and prepare for her inevitable shot. I play the move from her twelve point to my five point.

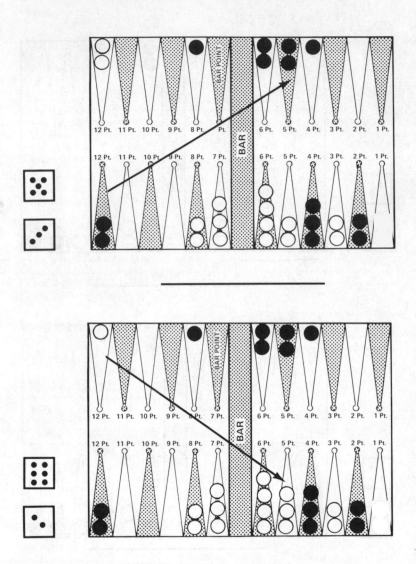

6—2: The best I can do is to bring my man from Lee's twelve to my five point leaving a blot. At least she doesn't have a strong board yet.

5—4: The four is for sure. I make my four point, gladly. Since I must have more men to work with, I move a five from Sara's four point to her nine point. My timing looks pretty good.

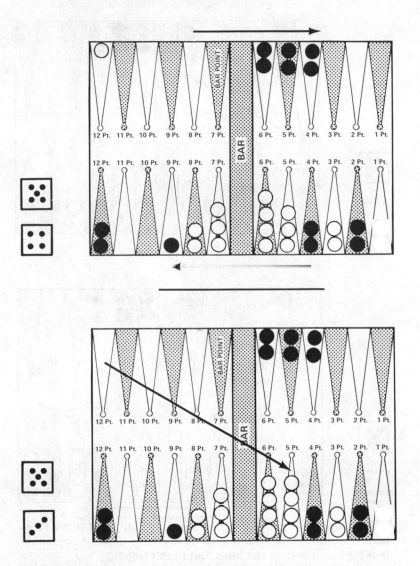

5—3: Safe again. My man comes home to my five point, but my troubles have just begun.

6—2: I definitely won't bring a man out of Sara's board since my shot is coming. I play the six to my bar, since it's the next important point for me, and the two to my eleven point.

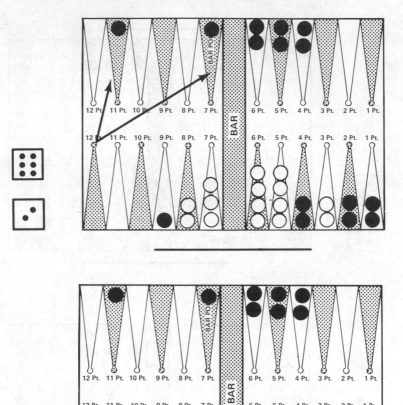

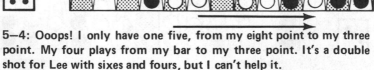

5—4: Ooops! I only have one five, from my eight point to my three point. My four plays from my bar to my three point. It's a double shot for Lee with sixes and fours, but I can't help it.

Lee's comments:

Hmmm-yummy ... Some people would double in this position. Can't blame them, but I'd like to hit or, if not, make my bar preparing for a later shot or two. A classic position for me and I feel a happy favorite at worst.

138

CHAPTER VIII

THE WONDERFUL WORLD
OF BACKGAMMON TOURNAMENTS

There have been game tournaments (bridge, chess, golf, tennis, etc.) held around the world for centuries, but none seem to have captured the imagination as much as backgammon tournaments.

Perhaps it's because of the exotic and romantic sounding places where they're held, such as Nassau, Grand Bahamas, Athens, London, St. Martin, San Juan, Aruba, Monte Carlo and Biarritz, or because of the wealth and glamor of the people who attend them, including stars such as Diana Ross and Polly Bergen and the famous rich such as Barry Gordy, the R. J. Reynolds, the Goodriches and the Swifts, or the incredible size of the stakes being wagered — but one thing's for sure, the popularity of backgammon and backgammon tournaments is growing faster than Topsy did.

A tournament usually lasts from five to seven days and I figure that an initial investment to attend one outside of the United States is about $1200 per person which includes room, meals, tips, travel expenses, entry fee and the cost of "buying yourself."

Everybody arrives about the same time for the "Auction" banquet where we pay our entry fee and people bid on you. In order to get money from winning, you have to bid on yourself or buy a part of yourself back from someone who "bought" you.

The entry fees vary according to your class and the scope of the tournament. Typical fees are: Beginners $75, Intermediate $150 and Championship $225.

The whole event is highly social. The actual tournament play is from 3 to 7 p.m. Mornings are for sleeping, water skiing, lying on the beach or general messing around.

This year I came back from Aruba with a great tan, some nice money and two giant bags of unusual and exquisite sea shells which are probably worth more than I won.

Before and after each day's tournament play, we play private games for money all over — on the beaches, in the clubs and even floating in the pools.

The stakes are anywhere from $5 a point to $50 in most games although there are usually a few games being played for as much as $1000 a point. When you count the doubling cube, there are games with as much as eight or even sixteen thousand dollars riding on them.

The most lost (outside of the tournament play) that I've ever been around was just under $200,000. That's a lot of money even for a millionaire to lose.

As far as tournament play goes, it varies enormously according to the auction, but I've seen many games where you could win as much as $30,000.

The tournament itself is usually held in the largest room in the hotel. Dress is casual: beach clothes, jeans, shorts, etc.

At most tournaments there are about 300 players with about 100 to 150 in the championship class. There are also perhaps another 500 who are there just for the social action.

The tables are long, with from 10 to 20 boards on each table. Behind the players and seated on each side are the kibitzers, but they're not allowed to talk at all. There are no referees, unless you ask for one.

You keep your own tally and as soon as you've won the match, you report your results to the tournament director (usually my good friend Alfred Sheinwold, the internationally renowned bridge columnist. Probably about 60% of the good backgammon players are also good bridge players).

A 15 point match usually starts the tournament and the final match is at least 25 points — and they're getting longer all the time. With luck such an important element, it takes at least 25 points to find which of two close players is really superior. I encourage much longer matches than 25; 35 would be a more valid test of skill.

The tournament director posts the results on the bracket sheets which are large and tacked to the wall.

If you've won, you look on the bracket sheet to see who you play next and if you don't know the person, he is paged over the mike.

After each day's play, people rest, get stoned and dress for dinner. The hotels serve lavish dinners and banquets every night of tournament play. After dinner, people play in the casinos, go dancing, play more backgammon or get into some sort of mischief. Few of us ever go to bed before five in the morning. After a week's vacation playing in a backgammon tournament, you usually need a week in bed.

If you think you're ready to play in a tournament or just want to attend one, write to the very fast growing World Backgammon Club, 30 East 68th Street, New York, New York 10022 and apply for membership. Their newsletters will keep you posted on all upcoming backgammon tournaments all over the world. Membership as of this writing is $35 a year. Membership gives you a reduced entry fee, specific invitations to all the tournaments, and all publications in regard to Backgammon.

"Gather ye match points while ye may."

TOURNAMENTS VS. HEAD-TO-HEAD PLAY:

The phrase "head-to-head play" refers to matches other than tournaments. The game strategy must be adjusted to suit the type of match you are involved in.

In a tournament match you are attempting to reach a specific number of points. Because of that, you take certain measures to win the match, especially to win a gammon in a crucial situation.

The Crawford rule, which is used in tournament play, states that if one player reaches match point (one point away from winning the match), there is no doubling by either opponent for that game and that game only. For example:

	YOU	YOUR OPPONENT
7 point	1	2
match	3	3
	4	5
	5	6 "match point"

Your opponent has accumulated six points, that is, has reached match point. Therefore, the Crawford Rule now applies. In the above match, your opponent needs only to win

141

one point, so he is not involved in trying to win a gammon. You, however, would happily play for a gammon if possible to end the match. Since losing the game means losing the match, you may make daring plays in a losing position since losing a gammon game is irrelevant.

Once the Crawford game has been played, the Holland Rule goes into effect if your opponent did not win the match. Now, either side may double on all following games until one player wins the match. However, neither side may double until each player has made two moves. This rule prevents the player who is behind in the match from doubling on the first roll and thereby making it difficult for his opponent to make an intelligent decision on whether to accept or reject the double.

Longer tournament matches lessen the luck element. I encourage them whenever time will allow. In a short match of 7 to 11 points, the mighty may fall by a quick run of good rolls by the lucky novice.

Your strategy with the doubling cube is generally more conservative than it would be in head-to-head play. You can't afford gammons in short matches, thus your takes are solid and you give up the cube with some caution.

If you are playing a match and find yourself behind considerably, you double early with a slight lead. Conversely, your opponent, well ahead in the match, does not give up possession of the cube unless his position is very sound. Obviously, if you were behind, say 9 to 2 in an 11 point match, and your opponent doubled you, you would take and turn the cube back to four at your first opportunity even though you may be a great underdog. You may get lucky and punish his error with a win.

Too Good to Double

In certain positions your game is so strong that doubling wins only one point since your opponent cannot possibly accept the double. To increase your plus expectation, you play for a gammon unless it becomes treacherous to do so — in which case you double as soon as the position is no longer a gammon position.

Jacoby Rule

The Jacoby Rule, designed for head-to-head play only, states that you may only win a gammon once the cube has been doubled. The purpose is to eliminate the boredom of obvious gammons on the one level. The practice is optional and should be determined prior to play.

CHAPTER IX

HOME TOURNAMENTS

In addition to the possibility of holding a backgammon tournament in your town, I suggest that you try a home tournament which we have found very entertaining among our friends.

Very little preparation is needed for the event. You will need a bracket sheet, illustrated below (which can be drawn or obtained from your local tennis shop), backgammon boards (which your guests will bring) and scoring paper and pencils.

Generally, knock-out matches are desirable, so if you are able to have the proper number of players (8, 16, 32, or 64, etc.) the movement will play evenly without "byes." Byes occur when the number of players is less than the perfect set. They may be given randomly by a draw or the players may be "seeded" (the best players) based on their ability to play or based on the amount they are sold for in an auction if you choose to run a Calcutta (a procedure which will be described later on). A player who receives a "bye" automatically wins that match and graduates to the next round as shown in the bracket diagram.

STARTING THE TOURNAMENT:

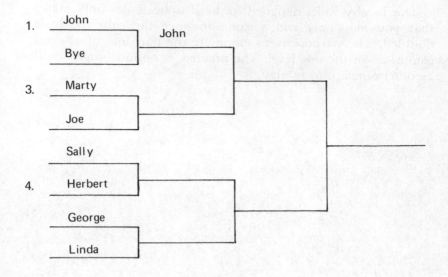

Once the bracket is arranged, matches may begin. The length of the matches is determined by the amount of time available for the entire event. The longer the matches, the higher degree of skill involved, but since often only one afternoon or evening is available, I suggest that the matches be to about seven points or less for the first few rounds and then increased to nine and eleven points respectively in the semi-final and final rounds. Winners play winners in each bracket until the movement is complete.

For those persons who lose in the first round, it is fun to hold a consolation flight so that everyone can continue to play longer. To do this you simply repeat the original procedure using all the defeated players and start the consolation rounds simultaneously with the second round of the championship flight.

An added attraction that my friends enjoy is a plaque I had engraved called "Backgammon Superstars" with each week's winners' names. This plaque is coveted by the new champion until he loses. This is especially nice if money is not involved in your tournament.

It is necessary to explain proper tournament rules to all participants prior to play. The following describes the basic rules:

1. Proper roll
   a. No cocked dice allowed — they must land flat on the board only.
   b. Each player rolls his dice on the side of the board to his right and both dice must land on the proper side to constitute a proper roll.
   c. A player may not roll his dice until his opponent has completed his move and picked up his dice from the board.
   d. Each player must use only one hand in moving his men around the board.

2. Crawford Rule

   No player may double his opponent when the match reaches game point. Example — if the match is to be played to seven points, as soon as one player has won six points, no one may double for the next game only. Therefore, that game is played for only one point, but if no one wins the match all following games can be doubled by either player until one player reaches seven points.

3. No automatic doubles.

4. One level (undoubled) gammons are counted in match play.

5. No settlements.

6. Should any questions regarding rules come up during the play, the players should call the director of the tournament to settle any disputes.

7. Scoring example — seven point match.

Stan	Tom
1	1
2	5
4	6 — game point
	7 — winner

145

A "Calcutta" is an auction of the players held prior to the start of the tournament. Players and guests may bid on the players they think most likely to win the tournament and all proceeds of the auction constitute the player pool. If, for example, you bid $5 to buy John and he, prior to play, asks to buy back 50% of himself, he pays you $2.50. Then, if he wins the tournament (let's say first prize is $50), you as half-owner win $25 and John wins $25. I think this adds excitement and interest although it is not a necessary part of the tournament and you do need to become aware of the gambling laws in your state in regard to this procedure.

The Calcutta may provide a method of seeding the players based on who was auctioned off for the highest amounts. As shown in the bracket diagram, the top four players would be placed on the chart where indicated, with the theory that they would be most likely to meet in the final rounds of the tournament. For the purpose of friendly home tournaments, I think that you need only to seed players one through four and draw the other players into the remaining spots.

In the case of prize money, below is an example of distribution. If we assume the total amount of the pool to be $100 you may divide it as follows:

Championship Flight	Consolation Flight
70% = $70.00	30% = $30.00
1st- 40% = $40.	1st- 20% = $20.
2nd-20% = $20.	2nd- 10% = $10.
3rd- 5% = $ 5.	$30.
4th- 5% = $ 5.	
$70.	

Another way of providing prize money is to charge an entry fee to each player and divide it as shown above.

Before you play a tournament, refer to Chapter VII regarding match techniques.

CHAPTER X

THE "CHOUETTE"
or
"What to do when company comes"

Backgammon is a game of two opposing sides, but not necessarily of only two players. When there are three or more players you use the "chouette" (shoe-ette) method of play. In a chouette, one player plays alone against a team composed of all the remaining players. The person playing alone is called "the box" and the player rolling the dice for the team is called "the captain." The game is played exactly the same as a head-to-head game with the following exceptions:

1) The captain has the final decision for all moves for the team.
2) If the box doubles, any player on the team may pass and concede the lower stake. The player or players who accept the double then play on for the higher stakes. If the captain passes a double, the next player in line may take it, thus becoming the new captain, and play the box.

Consulting vs. non-consulting chouettes — A chouette is generally played in what is called a consulting manner. The team may discuss among themselves how to take any move. In a non-consulting chouette, the captain must decide how to take all moves without aid from his partners. However, all players still have the option to accept or pass any double made by the box.

There is no limit to the number of players in a chouette, but generally, if there are six or more, the box becomes a two-man team with the same rules governing their side as the side of the captain. It is generally good strategy to play conservatively when "in the box" as one big loss will make it impossible to end the evening as a winner. Conversely, playing on the team side, you might accept a double slightly more freely as you do not have as much to lose.

147

Scoring the chouette — Scoring is the same as regular play, except that since the player in the box is playing against a team of players, he loses or wins the amount of the stake from each player on the team. Therefore, if a game ends and the box wins a two game against three players, the box wins six points and each team member loses two each.

Chouettes are a great way to advance your backgammon skills, since there are generally one or more better players in the game and you can benefit from their knowledge.

Also, chouettes are very exciting because everybody is constantly screaming out their idea of the correct move. Hence, the translation of the French word "chouette" is "screech owl." Try it — you'll like it!

Regular backgammon is so interesting that you will never tire of the standard game but just for kicks try one of the following variations:

THE PIN GAME:

In the pin game, when you hit a blot it does not go to the bar but stays locked in place under your man until you lift all men off the blot and free your opponent's man to move. The basic objective of the game is the same as in standard backgammon, with the first player removing all his men from the board in the bear-off being the winner. There is no doubling cube and the scoring is done by counting the number of pips that the loser has remaining on the board. For example, if the loser has one man left on his four point and one on his six point, he has ten pips left and loses ten points. If he fails to bear off even one man, as in standard backgammon, he has been gammoned and his pip total is doubled. If he fails to bear off one man and has one man or more still in his opponent's inner board, he is backgammoned and his pip total is trebled.

The starting position of the board in the pin game varies from standard backgammon. Each side starts with 13 men on your opponent's one point: one man on his eight point and one man on his ten point. Two of your men on a point or one of your men pinning one of your opponent's men creates a blocking point and, just as in standard backgammon, your opponent cannot land on that space.

148

ACEY-DUCEY:

The only difference between this variation and standard backgammon is that when a player rolls a one and a two on his throw of the dice, he takes the one, the two, a double number of his choice and then takes another roll.

BACKGAMMON TO LOSE:

You will probably play this variation of the game very infrequently, but it can be fun. It is played like standard backgammon and from the standard starting position. The only difference is that the object is to lose the game. You are not required to hit a blot unless that is the only legal way to take the move. It is best played with the doubling cube (if you think you are going to lose, you double). It is the only variation of the game where being backgammoned is fun.

BACKGAMMON FOR CHILDREN:

Since my children want to be involved in everything I do, and I do a lot of backgammon, I developed a simple variation for them. Instead of clamoring to roll my dice when I play, they now root for "boxcars" and "midnight" in their own game. The game is an excellent exercise in counting and my baby hustlers will be well prepared to deal with any croupier they happen to cross in their more mellow years.

Each player starts with four checkers, two on the one point and two on the three point, in their opponent's home board. From there the game proceeds using the same general rules as backgammon. The object is to bring your men home and bear them off. You may make points and hit blots and your primary concern is to race. When things go well you win a trip to the cookie jar — not a bad game for adults too, but a little fattening.

GLOSSARY

Automatic doubles. An optional rule designed for increasing the stakes by starting the doubling cube at two if both players roll the same number on the first roll.

Back Game. Often a result of a blot-hitting contest. This game is used when one player is considerably behind in the race and adopts the strategy of holding two or more points in his opponent's home board. His eventual goal is to hit a blot his opponent has been forced to leave while bearing in.

Backgammon. A win, which is scored as triple, because your opponent has left one or more men in your home board or on the bar at the time that you are able to bear off all of your men. This is counted only when your opponent has not taken any men off the board.

Back men. The two men which begin in your opponent's inner board, on the one point.

Bar. The center strip, usually raised, which separates the inner and outer quadrants or tables.

Bar point. Each player's seven point.

Bearing off. The process of removing your men from your inner board at the end of the game.

Beaver. An optional gambling maneuver which allows the person being doubled to immediately re-double the cube, keeping possession of it.

Blocking game. A game in which the player builds several adjacent points in an attempt to trap his opponent's men.

Blot. A single man on a point. Also called an "exposed man" since it is vulnerable to being hit by one of your opponent's men and sent to the bar.

150

Board. The entire backgammon table or one of the four quadrants within the table.

Box. In a chouette, the player who rolled the highest number at the start of the game is the "man in the box." He plays alone against a team of all the other players. After each game the man in the box is the winner of the previous game.

Boxcars. Slang term for double sixes; also called "midnight."

Break a prime. To remove a man or men from a row of six consecutive points.

Builder. A blot or extra man on a point which is in position to be used to create another point.

Captain. In a chouette, the leader of the team playing against the box. The captain rolls the dice and has the final decision on what moves to make and when to double.

Chouette. A variation of backgammon for three or more players. One person plays alone against a team of the other players who are led by the captain.

Closed board. If all six points on a player's inner board have two or more men on them, then an opponent's man on the bar cannot re-enter.

Cocked dice. Thrown dice that have not landed flat on one side of the board and must be re-tossed.

Combination shot. A blot that is more than six points away from one of your men. It takes a combination of the numbers on both dice to be able to hit it.

Come in. To bring a man from the bar to your opponent's inner or home board.

Consolation flight. In a tournament, another tournament run for those who lost their first match.

Contact. A position in which there is still a possibility of leaving a blot.

Count the position. The pip count of both players is totaled in a running game to determine who has the advantage.

Cube. See "doubling cube."

Direct shot. A blot that is within a six point range of your opponent's man. It may be hit by a specific number on a single die.

Double. Doubling the stakes of the game.

Doubles or doublets. A roll with the same number on both dice. It is played by moving a total of four times the number on one die.

Doubling cube. The large "fifth" die in your backgammon set. Its faces are numbered with 2, 4, 8, 16, 32 and 64. It is used to double the stakes of the game.

Gammon. A gammon occurs when your opponent has taken off all of his men and you have yet to take off any men. It is scored as double the stakes of the game.

Hit. To land on your opponent's blot and send the man to the bar.

Home board. Your inner board with the points numbered one through six. Your object is to bring all of your men to your inner or home board before you bear them off.

Inner board. See "home board."

Lover's leap. In backgammon jargon, another name for an opening roll of 6-5.

Making a point. Placing two or more men on one point, blocking your opponent from legally landing on or touching down on that point.

Outer board. The quadrant adjacent to your home board. It is numbered with points seven through twelve.

Pip. Another name for a point. It is a term generally used in counting a position.

Point. Any of the twenty-four triangles on the board. In this book, they are numbered one through twelve on either side of the board.

Point on a blot. To hit an opponent's man with two of your men on the same roll.

Position. The way the men are placed on the board.

Prime. Six consecutive points on the board. A man trapped behind a prime cannot escape until the prime is broken.

Redouble. Doubling after the game has been doubled.

Running game. A game in which there is no longer a possibility of contact. This game will be won by the player who rolls the highest number of pips.

TABLES OF PROBABILITY AND ODDS

The Number Of Ways Of Hitting A Blot

There isn't a game of backgammon played where you don't have to decide between two (or more) places where you should leave a blot. Normally you want to leave it on a point where it is least likely to be hit. The rule of thumb is that if your choice is between a 6 and a smaller number, take the smaller number; and if it is between a 7 and a larger number, take the larger number. You could memorize the following table, but it is laid out here so that you can easily understand the principle in counting the number of ways you can be hit, from one point away to 24 points away (double 6 is the largest throw). Knowing this table by heart will put you in the expert league. Knowing how to figure it on your own will put you in the expert league too, but will make you a slower player.

Points Away	Singles	Combinations	Doubles	Number of throws which can hit
1	11 1's			11
2	11 2's		1111	12
3	11 3's	(1-2)(2-1)	1111	14
4	11 4's	(1-3)(3-1)	1111,2222	15
5	11 5's	(1-4)(4-1)(2-3)(3-2)		15
6	11 6's	(1-5)(5-1)(2-4)(4-2)	2222,3333	17
7		(1-6)(6-1)(2-5)(5-2)(3-4)(4-3)		6
8		(2-6)(6-2)(3-5)(5-3)	2222,4444	6
9		(3-6)(6-3)(4-5)(5-4)	3333	5
10		(4-6)(6-4)	5555	3
11		(5-6)(6-5)		2
12			3333,4444,6666	3
13				0
14				0
15			5555	1
16			4444	1
17				0
18			6666	1
19				0
20			5555	1
21				0
22				0
23				0
24			6666	1

154

TABLES OF PROBABILITY AND ODDS

Probability Of Hitting A Blot

(Assuming no enemy's points have been made between you and the blot)

Points Away	No. of throws which can hit	Percentage of hitting	Odds against hitting
1	11	31%	25 to 11
2	12	33%	2 to 1
3	14	39%	11 to 7
4	15	42%	7 to 5
5	15	42%	7 to 5
6	17	47%	19 to 17
7	6	17%	5 to 1
8	6	17%	5 to 1
9	5	14%	31 to 5
10	3	8%	11 to 1
11	2	6%	17 to 1
12	3	8%	11 to 1
15	1	3%	35 to 1
16	1	3%	35 to 1
18	1	3%	35 to 1
20	1	3%	35 to 1
24	1	3%	35 to 1

TABLES OF PROBABILITY AND ODDS

Probability of Entering From The Bar

When you have a man on the bar, your chances are better than even that you'll come in on the next roll, unless there is only one point open. For a complete breakdown, see below:

Number of points open	Ways to come in	Percentage of coming in	Odds for or against
1	11	31%	25 to 11 against
2	20	56%	5 to 4 for
3	27	75%	3 to 1 for
4	32	89%	8 to 1 for
5	35	97%	35 to 1 for

TABLES OF PROBABILITY AND ODDS

Probability of Bearing Off the Last One or Two Men in the Last One or Two Rolls

Where you place your last few men while bearing off can be very crucial. For example, if you have a man on the 6 point and a man on the 5 point, and you role a 1-2, where do you put them? You could double up on the four point, or put men on the 5 and 3 points, or the 6 and 2 points. See below for the answer to this and other similar problems.

Total Points	Your Man or Men are on the following points	Number of Winning throws	Percentage of winning (one roll)	Percentage of winning (two rolls)
12	6-6	4	11%	78%
11	6-5	6	17%	88%
10	5-5	6	17%	92%
	6-4	8	22%	93%
9	5-4	10	28%	96%
	6-3	10	28%	97%
8	4-4	11	31%	98%
	6-2	13	36%	99%
	5-3	14	39%	99%
7	6-1	15	42%	99%
	4-3	17	47%	99%
	5-2	19	53%	99%
6	3-3	17	47%	100%
	5-1 or 4-2	23	64%	100%
	6	27	75%	100%
5	3-2	25	69%	100%
	4-1	29	81%	100%
	5	31	86%	100%
4	2-2	26	72%	100%
	3-1 or 4	34	94%	100%
3	2-1 or 3	36	100%	100%
2	1-1 or 2	36	100%	100%

TABLES OF PROBABILITY AND ODDS

There are 36 possible combinations of rolls on the dice in backgammon. They are:

Double 1	1
Double 2	1
Double 3	1
Double 4	1
Double 5	1
Double 6	1
1-2, 2-1	2
1-3, 3-1	2
1-4, 4-1	2
1-5, 5-1	2
1-6, 6-1	2
2-3, 3-2	2
2-4, 4-2	2
2-5, 5-2	2
2-6, 6-2	2
3-4, 4-3	2
3-5, 5-3	2
3-6, 6-3	2
4-5, 5-4	2
4-6, 6-4	2
5-6, 6-5	2
	36

A Cliff House— P/S/S Book